THE SAXOPHONE REED

The Advanced Art of
Adjusting Single Reeds

Written and Illustrated
by Ray Reed

First Edition
October 2004

ISBN 978-0-7414-2305-4

Published by:

INFINITY
PUBLISHING.COM

1094 New De Haven Street, Suite 100
West Conshohocken, PA 19428-2713
Info@buybooksontheweb.com
www.buybooksontheweb.com
Toll-free (877) BUY BOOK
Local Phone (610) 941-9999
Fax (610) 941-9959

∞

Printed in the United States of America
Printed on Recycled Paper
Published March 2015

Foreword by Bob Irvine

The Saxophone Reed - The Advanced Art of Adjusting Single Reeds provides the definitive technical-reference source material needed by serious professional musicians and music students who seek near perfection in the art and craft of reed adjustments. This book could only have been written by a master multi-reed instrumentalist with a strong technical background and the perseverance to investigate, analyze, and document the results of his findings. This book is a life work of the master musician, composer, arranger, graphic artist, and now published author, Ray Reed, who has invested over thirty-five years of research and on-the-job experience in its production. Reed has succeeded in demystifying the unpredictable natural characteristics of mass-produced cane reeds and has provided a scientific approach to preparing reeds for optimum performance. Commercial reed manufacturers can benefit from this book by more fully understanding the problems musicians experience with mass-produced reeds and the processes required by serious musicians to achieve full-quality performance.

This book was written entirely by the author and is presented with pride as written without the need for editing by others. All text, tables, illustrations, layouts, and cover design were solely prepared and generated by the author on his personal computer at home. The extensive Table of Contents is formatted for ease of reference and is supported by headings on the upper corners of each page throughout the book.

First and foremost, I would like to thank Ray Reed for just being my special friend, and to thank him for the opportunity and honor of allowing the RBI Enterprises - Arts Division to support the publication of this book.

Our company is also executive producer of the companion CD to this book, The Ray Reed Quintet - *Once Upon a Reed*. This CD provides living proof of the exceptional response that reed instrumentalists may achieve through the technology provided in this book. This is Ray's debut album as a leader of an all-star straight-ahead jazz quintet with Ray Reed-Alto Sax, Carl Saunders-Trumpet, Tom Garvin-Piano, Tom Warrington-Bass, and Joe La Barbera-Drums. The six fresh, new jazz compositions by Ray and two timeless standards on this album provide vehicles to demonstrate the excellent sound qualities that can be achieved with optimized reeds in the hands of a master musician. This CD is receiving rave reviews worldwide and is available from Sea Breeze Jazz (SB-3065) and from most on-line sources, record stores, and book stores.

The RBI Enterprises - Arts Division is dedicated to the development, promotion, and preservation of art in the forms of jazz music, fine art in most media, and the publication of related books and literature. ***The Saxophone Reed - The Advanced Art of Adjusting Single Reeds*** is the first major publication supported by our organization and a work in which we take extreme pride. For more information or new projects, please email: bobjass@aol.com.

Bob Irvine - President
RBI Enterprises - Arts Division

Sea Breeze Jazz SB-3065

Encino, California
January 1994

Fellow Saxophonists:

Nearly every player has experimented with clipping and scraping reeds. And although some success may have been gained, the real nature of what makes a reed play has probably evaded most people. Nevertheless, the principles that govern reed performance are genuine and consistent. And whether these principles are to be partially applied or fully applied, your reeds should play better and last longer than any unadjusted factory cuts that you can find.

One area of concern is the natural warping of reed backs. Reeds are continually modulating between their static and dynamic shapes, and the results of these motions are destructive air leaks between the reeds and the mouthpiece. This book will explain how to minimize these problems with the reeds, but it is not our purpose here to level your mouthpiece for you. So keep looking for a better mouthpiece. And if you find one, be sure that the bed and lower rails are reasonably flat.

Also, remember that dry summer heat (over 90 degrees) can promote extreme warping action in a reed. So to ensure the best chance of success with this project, wait until a milder season before becoming deeply involved in these procedures.

Ray Reed

idig

PREFACE

All reeds are individual objects; and to achieve uniform performance qualities from them, they must be treated as such. That is, if all reeds for a specific mouthpiece were cut to the same dimensions, proportions, and thicknesses, they would all display differences in tone quality, strength, and intonation. These differences would be caused by material variations in each piece of cane; such as, density, grain structure, and warping tendencies.

Figure 1

LENGTHWISE AREA DIVISIONS

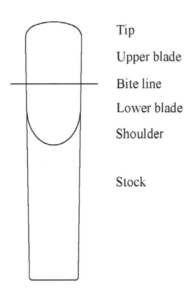

Tip

Upper blade

Bite line

Lower blade

Shoulder

Stock

Consistency and Inconsistency

Consistency in the Upper Blade

The playing qualities of reeds will, however, also display similarities of which the player can take great advantage. Specifically, the upper blades of all new reeds comprised of medium-density cane can be matched in thickness and taper. These matchings will produce reeds with uniform tone qualities.

Inconsistency in the Lower Blade and Stock

When the upper blade has been correctly cut, the detrimental playing qualities of a new reed can usually (but not always) be traced to the lower blade and stock. The greater proportion of wood in these combined areas, compared to the upper blade, is the major factor determining the strength and pitch of the reed. Also, since these areas anchor the upper blade in its vibrating position, further refinements in tone quality are possible by modifying these two lower areas.

Break-In Sessions

Static and Dynamic Shapes

When a reed is placed into vibration, tremendous stresses are placed on its fibers; and as a result of these stresses, the reed will quickly change from its static shape (resting shape) to its dynamic shape (playing shape). Although some cutting can be done while the reed is in its static shape, complete balancing must be done while the reed is in its dynamic shape.

Dynamic Balancing of the Lower Blade and Stock

Most of the shape changing occurs in the lower areas because of the abundance of wood there, and the factory always leaves this wood in a condition of extreme imbalance. Dynamic balancing requires the massive removal of wood from the lower areas to minimize air leaks and to regulate the amount of ringing in the sound.

The need for repeated break-in sessions. No matter how thoroughly the lower areas are balanced on the first playing session, the internal tension of the fibers will pull the reed back into its full static shape when it is allowed to rest for several hours. And when the reed is vibrated into its dynamic shape on the next playing session, the air leaks will return and require additional recutting of the lower areas. This time, however, the air leaks will not be as severe as during the preceding session; and less rebalancing will be needed (although there will be exceptions).

This process will be repeated, requiring less recutting during each playing session, until the reed stabilizes or until the player otherwise determines that the reed is ready for performance.

Expansion and Water Absorption

Expansion. Vibrated cane will display a swelling action that affects each reed in its own unique way. When this happens, an upper blade that has been precut to exact specifications will reveal random areas that are now too thick. The thick areas will prevent the left and right sides of the upper blade from bending and vibrating evenly, and the tone will therefore become distorted. Also, the swelling action can affect the blending of the reed tip into the upper heart, resulting in various other problems.

Water absorption. Since water is an integral part of the reed, its weight should be evenly distributed between the left and right sides of the upper blade. When only one side of the upper blade is too thick, whether through vibration expansion or through miscutting, it will contain a greater weight of water than the opposite side. This condition results in further tone distortion due to inertia imbalance as the reed vibrates at hundreds of times per second.

Controlling the expansion. The rate and degree of expansion for a new reed cannot be predicted, but it can be controlled by thinning the upper blade back to its original specifications at the end of each short break-in session. And unlike the static/dynamic/static shaping cycle of the lower areas, vibration expansion in the reed blade will usually remain when the reed has been dried and rested.[*]

---

[*]*The vibration expansion of a new reed can often be used to an advantage. This situation exists when the manufacturer creates a reed that area is too thin, and the expansion will increase the area toward the correct thickness.*

When To Cut Reeds

Cutting and balancing should be done as early in the reed life as possible as this parallels the reed tendencies to warp and swell the greatest amounts during its earliest minutes and hours of play. If the initial balancing is delayed for too many playing hours, there is a good chance that removing large amounts of wood will destroy the reed. Touching up reeds, though, can be successful well into the reed life; particularly, if a reed has been fully balanced in its early hours of play.

Fully Balanced Reeds and Quick-Cut Reeds

Fully Balanced Reeds

The emphasis of this book is to create fully balanced reeds because this allows the most complete discussion of the forces that control all single reeds. Fully balanced reeds also offer the greatest performance qualities that a player can experience. But no matter how wonderfully these reeds can be made to play, there is one substantial problem in their development. The problem is that producing and maintaining an adequate supply takes too much time.

Quick-cut reeds, however, can be rapidly produced.

Quick-Cut Reeds

A quick-cut reed is simply a factory-cut reed that has been placed through one or two short break-in sessions before being used for performance. These reeds will outplay factory cuts nearly every time because they will be at least partially balanced on your mouthpiece while the reeds are in their dynamic shapes, which is something the factory cannot do for you. The cutting and balancing required for quick-cut reeds are easily accomplished (some reeds, though, will present more difficult problems), and further adjustments are usually possible at a later time. Also, quick-cut reeds may be the best solution for a player who is short on patience but nevertheless desires to play on better reeds.

Reed-Working Tools and Player Temperament

Reed-Working Tools

When the mechanics of vibration are thoroughly understood, reeds may be successfully adjusted with easy-to-use tools like files and sandpaper. But however skillfully these tools may be applied, imbalances are likely to remain in each reed. Furthermore, the upper blades of all new reeds will not be closely matched, which introduces a margin of confusion to the player.

To produce closely matched, balanced upper blades, the dial indicator and reed knife have proved to be the most efficient tools.

The dial indicator. This is a clockwork-type micrometer that is used in conjunction with a measuring gridwork.[*] And as a reed is positioned at each gridwork intersection, the measurement for that reed area is displayed on the dial face. The advantage of this measuring tool is that the various curves of the reed blade can be analyzed and adjusted with far greater accuracy than eyesight and intuition would otherwise allow.

The reed knife. The reed knife is recommended as the most versatile and accurate tool for adjusting reed blades. The reason for its superiority is the unbeveled cutting edge that is perfectly straight from the handle to the blade tip. A knife shaped in this fashion will automatically seek high spots on the reed surface and will powder them down to specifications without accidentally cutting into adjacent areas. The reed knife is particularly suited for removing exact amounts of wood and is the ideal companion for the dial indicator. A medium-light (or light) cutting stroke applied to a small, average area of the reed blade will remove about 1 ten-thousandth of an inch (.0001 inch) of wood. This means that 5 strokes will remove 1/2 thousandth of an inch (.0005 inch), 10 strokes will remove 1 thousandth of an inch (.001 inch), and so on. The result of this cutting is that reed upper blades can be balanced to tolerances of less than 1/2 thousandth of an inch in thickness.

Player Temperament and the Reed Knife

Some players, though, for whatever their reasons will be averse to using the reed knife. And these players will be better suited by using an alternate cutting tool, such as,

---

[*]*Construction of the micrometer assembly is discussed in the appendix on page 141.*

a file. Filed blades can produce excellent reeds because the resulting surfaces will be very smooth. The smoothness ensures that the blade areas are blending together correctly and that miniature stress risers,[*] which usually result from the exclusive use of the reed knife, are eliminated.

Player Temperament and the Dial Indicator

Many players may also feel apprehensive about the dial indicator, perhaps being unwilling to endure the tedium involved in its use. But reed cutting does not necessarily need to be complicated (although it certainly can be if you allow it). And most players should find the dial indicator to be an immense benefit, even if it is used only to balance the upper edges and tips of quick-cut reeds.

The Major Criteria

The State of Equilibrium

As physical imbalances are removed from a reed, it will evolve to a state of equilibrium. This state is characterized by the even distribution of stress loads and by each reed area cooperating with the actions of the others.

The state of equilibrium is desirable in a reed, but remember that a well-balanced reed is nothing more than a precisely shaped piece of wood. It is the player's ability to create music with it that is most important. And from the player's requirements to make music, the qualities of tone, strength, and intonation will emerge as the major criteria that determine the success or failure of a reed.

Tone, Strength, and Intonation

These three qualities are an interdependent force group, which means that when one quality is adjusted, the character of the other two will also be changed.

Tone and strength in the upper blade. Although the lower areas of the reed provide the foundation of its stiffness, the upper blade must also contribute to the reed strength. Otherwise, the upper blade would simply collapse against the mouthpiece tip

---

[*]*A discussion of stress risers is found on page 65.*

rail. And even though the upper-blade function is to establish the tone quality, the interdependent quality of stiffness must be considered in the upper-blade design as shown below.

TONE QUALITY AND THE RELATIVE
STIFFNESS OF THE UPPER BLADE

Tone Quality	Relative Stiffness
Excess buzzing	Extra stiff
Reduced buzzing	Stiff
Clear tone	Medium
Clearer tone	Weak
Rattling	Extra weak

Variations in tone and strength. Because of the individual nature of each piece of cane, finished reeds will display slight differences in tone and strength. But if these variations are within the ranges that are acceptable to the player, then the tone and strength may be considered to be correctly expressed in the reed.

Consistency in intonation. Intonation, on the other hand, is a rigid specification that is not subject to artistic interpretation. And all intonation problems must be adjusted even though the tone and strength will be changed as a result.

Adjustments for intonation. The general rule for adjusting intonation is that:

1. REMOVING WOOD FROM THE BLADE WILL LOWER THE PITCH WHILE WEAKENING THE STRENGTH AND REDUCING THE BUZZ IN THE TONE; AND

2. ADDING WOOD TO THE BLADE (BY CLIPPING THE TIP) WILL RAISE THE PITCH WHILE INCREASING THE STRENGTH AND ADDING BUZZ TO THE TONE.

<u>Closing</u>

Most players are aware of the intonation-adjustment rule but may have experienced undependable results from its application. This is because tone, strength, and intonation are only some of the forces operating in a reed. There are others of which the player may have been unaware. And since these forces operate simultaneously, they are all the interdependent among one another. In dealing with these compound adjustments, an advantage will be found in creating dynamically balanced reeds; particularly, those comprised of responsive, medium-density cane. When these conditions are met, the adjustments needed will become more obvious and their effects more predictable.

Also, since these compound adjustments involve the lengthwise proportions of wood throughout the various reed areas, then lengthwise-oriented thinking should simplify the adjustment process.

❖   ❖   ❖

TABLE OF CONTENTS

Section   Page

Section   Page

Section   Page

Section   Page

❖   ❖   ❖

LIST OF ILLUSTRATIONS

Illustration   Page

Illustration   Page

Illustration   Page

❖   ❖   ❖

LIST OF TABLES

Table   Page

❖   ❖   ❖

THE SAXOPHONE REED

The Advanced Art of
Adjusting Single Reeds

❖   ❖   ❖

I. CANE SYMMETRY

Equal Strength in the Blade Edges

The hardest wood in a cane tube is found in the bark. And as the cross section progresses toward the inner wall of the tube, the wood will become gradually softer.

Therefore, when a reed is cut from a round tube, the hard and soft areas will be distributed as shown in Illustration 1. This distribution ensures nearly equal strength in the blade edges when they are cut to equal thicknesses.

Illustration 1

DISTRIBUTION OF HARD AND SOFT AREAS

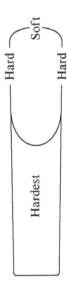

Crosswise Balancing of the Reed Shoulder

If a reed is cut slightly off center from the tube, the resulting imbalance of blade-edge hardness may not be critical to the reed performance. But if the off-center cutting (or a natural malformation of the tube) results in uneven shoulder thickness as shown in Illustrations 2a and 2b, then the stock must be filed down as shown in Illustrations 2c and 2d.

A balanced shoulder is necessary to avoid the crosswise displacement of the pivot point (see page 5), and it will also prevent the warping actions from gravitating around the thicker shoulder side.

When filing the stock in this procedure, do not allow the shoulder to become thinner than that of a normal reed, even though some crosswise imbalance might remain. In doing so, the lengthwise proportions of wood may become too imbalanced to repair.

Crosswise Balancing of the Lower Blade

If filing the stock in the above procedure produces a shoulder edge that is too high on the reed profile (too close to the reed tip) as shown in Illustrations 2e and 2f, then the lower blade on that same side is also too thick. And since this extra wood produces the same problems as a misbalanced shoulder, the lower blade must be cut down as shown in Illustrations 2g and 2h. Once again, do not allow the lower blade to become thinner than that of a normal reed.

Illustration 2

CROSSWISE BALANCING OF THE
SHOULDER AND LOWER BLADE

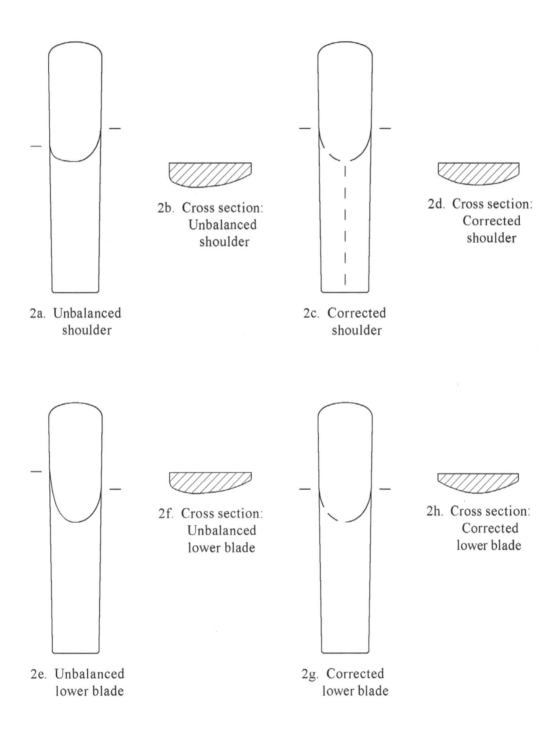

2a. Unbalanced
shoulder

2b. Cross section:
Unbalanced
shoulder

2c. Corrected
shoulder

2d. Cross section:
Corrected
shoulder

2e. Unbalanced
lower blade

2f. Cross section:
Unbalanced
lower blade

2g. Corrected
lower blade

2h. Cross section:
Corrected
lower blade

II. THE PIVOT POINT

The pivot point and pivot lines represent the wave-like motion of the blade as it vibrates from left to right and back again. The wave-like motion is generated by a floating center of pressure, created by the player's breath, combined with the spring action of the reed. Within this motion the center of pressure will move from one pivot line (or bending axis) to the next through a nearly infinite number of pivot lines.

The pivot point will always gravitate toward the thickest and stiffest area near the reed shoulder. And in a balanced reed this will be in the exact crosswise center.

However, if the shoulder or lower blade area is unbalanced, the pivot point will be drawn toward the thicker side of the reed. When this happens, the pivot lines will also be drawn off center; and the reed will play with uneven resistance.

Illustration 3

THE PIVOT POINT AND PIVOT LINES

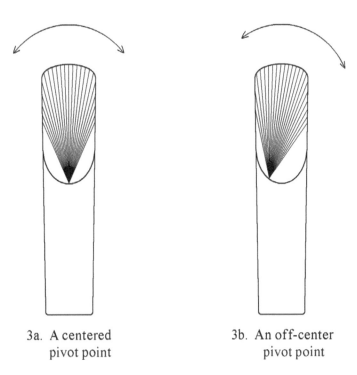

3a. A centered   3b. An off-center
     pivot point   pivot point

III. MATCHING THE REED TO THE EMBOUCHURE

The Bite Line

This is an arbitrary line that separates the upper blade from the lower blade.

The vertical position of the bite line (and therefore the length of the bite) can be slightly different for each new reed. But as a reed is adjusted and broken in, the bite line may be moved closer to the ideal location for your embouchure.

Illustration 4

THE BITE LINE

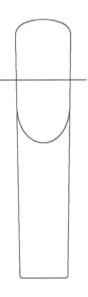

How the Bite-Line Position Is Established

The interdependent proportions of wood between the upper and lower blades determine the bite-line position as follows:

1. IF THE PROPORTIONS OF WOOD BETWEEN THE UPPER AND LOWER BLADES ARE BALANCED, THEN A NATURAL BITE WILL RESULT;

2. IF THE LOWER BLADE HAS SUFFICIENT WOOD TO OVERPOWER THE UPPER BLADE, THEN A SHORT BITE WILL RESULT; AND

3. IF THE LOWER BLADE HAS INSUFFICIENT WOOD AS COMPARED TO THE UPPER BLADE (OR IF THE SHOULDER EDGE IS TOO FAR AWAY FROM THE REED TIP), THEN A LONG BITE WILL RESULT.

Embouchure Distress and the Lower Blade

A long bite can cause the embouchure to begin pinching the reed in an effort to maintain an air seal. And as the bite becomes even longer through the actions of the primary and tangent warps,[1] the pinching action of the lower lip can cause extreme embouchure distress.

Adjusting the Bite-Line Position

Since the principal antagonist to the embouchure is the warp-induced air leak, the backside of the lower blade and stock must be reflattened (dynamically balanced) to restore a reasonable bite.

After the back has been reflattened, the bite line may be repositioned (if needed) by the following techniques:

1. The bite may be shortened by removing wood from the upper blade;

2. The bite may also be shortened by clipping the reed tip; and

3. The bite may be lengthened by removing wood from the lower blade (or by filing the shoulder edge).

The reason why the bite may need to be lengthened again is to balance other forces in the reed. And this lengthening should be cautiously approached to avoid the development or redevelopment of the lip-pinching problem; especially, before the reed shape has stabilized during the break-in process.

How the Bite-Line Adjustment Affects the Reed Strength

Removing wood from the blade front side will reduce the reed strength to some degree. But since this cutting will bring the reed into a closer state of equilibrium

---

[1] *The effects of the primary and tangent warps (which are detailed in the next section) are to move the reed lower edges away from the mouthpiece, thus creating potentially massive air leaks.*

These warps can cause embouchure discomfort with any length bite, but the effects are particularly severe with a bite that is already too long because of misbalancing in the proportions of wood in the upper and lower blades.

adapted to your mouthpiece and embouchure, the results should be satisfactory. If not, then too much wood was removed; or the cane was too soft.

The average reed of your usual strength should be able to withstand a few backside reflattenings, as required for quick-cut reeds, without the strength collapsing or the pitch going flat.

Full Balancing of Half-Strength-Harder Reeds

However, a more complete reduction of air leaks (and therefore greater embouchure comfort) as required for fully balanced reeds, will need even more wood removed from the backsides. And as a prerequisite, reeds that are one-half-strength harder may be selected. These reeds will play stiffly during the first few minutes of play. But as wood is removed during the adjustment process, the reeds will quickly evolve to the correct strength for your embouchure. If not, then this option must be declined.

Avoiding Extra-Stiff Reeds

If stiff reeds are already being used, then moving to a half-strength harder may prove to be detrimental. In this instance boxes of harder reeds may contain too many pieces of high-density cane. And high-density cane can be very unresponsive to adjustments, thus canceling the advantage of increasing the reed strength.

❖　　❖　　❖

IV. THE NATURAL WARPING ACTIONS

The Source of the Primary Warp

The single reed, being flat on one side and rounded on the other, is designed in a state of imbalance. That is, when a precise line is drawn between the highest and lowest points in the reed cross section, termed a centerline, a greater mass of wood will be found toward the flat side of the reed.

The distance between the centerline and the center of mass determines the amount of imbalance for an individual reed, and this imbalance is the source of the primary warp.

Illustration 5

CROSS SECTION: THE CENTERLINE
AND THE CENTER OF MASS

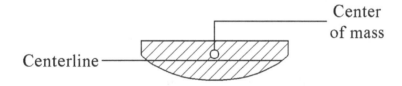

Development of the Primary Warp

First, consider a reed in its static shape, resting in a box. Then the reed is placed into vibration; and suddenly it is being furiously twisted, blasted by shock waves, and flooded with hot, lubricating fluid.

11

The reed, being made of a flexible material, will react to these forces in the only way possible. The fibers will adjust their positions to withstand the new environment (much as a handful of axially aligned pencils will adjust their positions when you manipulate your fist).

TO DISTRIBUTE THE STRESSES EVENLY, THE REED WILL

SEEK A MORE CLOSELY BALANCED SHAPE. AND A MORE

CLOSELY BALANCED SHAPE REQUIRES THE CENTER OF MASS

TO BE MOVED CLOSER TO THE CENTERLINE.

This means that mass from the flat side will be moved toward the curved side.

Since thinner cross section areas present less resistance to this motion, the reed edges will begin to curl away from the mouthpiece, creating progressively wider and longer edge gaps for air escapement (decompression) as the warp continues to develop. Also, note that the action becomes less severe as the blade thickness diminishes toward the reed tip edge where the center of mass and the centerline are in the exact, same place.

After the reed has been played for a few minutes, check the new elliptically shaped back with the straight edge as shown in Illustration 6.

With your visual sense trained on the contact point, the cross section will appear to have developed an outward bulge. But in reality the high point is in its original position; it is the edges that have retracted from their original positions. Nevertheless, thinking of it as a bulge is geometrically correct. And it is the bulge area that will be systematically reflattened (dynamically balanced) during the break-in process.

Illustration 6

CROSS SECTION: THE PRIMARY WARP I

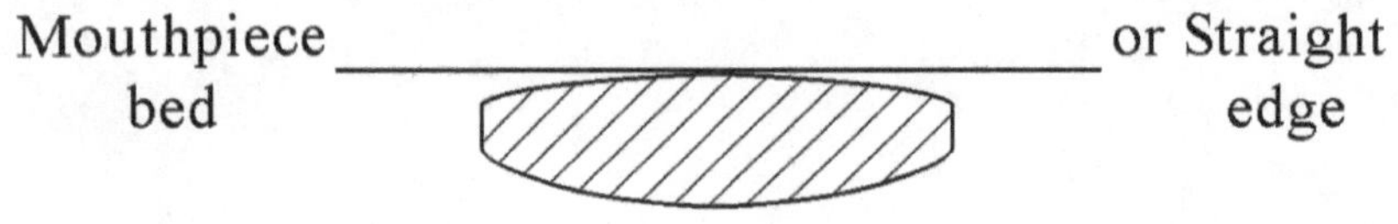

Mouthpiece _____ or Straight
bed   edge

Checking the Back for Warps

First, remove the excess water by drawing and rubbing the reed between the thumb and forefinger. This will make the edge gaps easier to see and will also allow for better control when cutting; then

To check for a crosswise warp, use a straight edge (a 6-inch metal ruler) and your desk lamp. With the reed flat side up, aim the stock right into the lamp, a few inches away from the bulb. Now rock and slide the straight edge along the flat side from the bite line to the middle of the stock (or sometimes beyond).

To check for a lengthwise warp, place the reed in its playing position on the mouthpiece and hold it there with your thumb on the stock. Aim the stock end of the assembly into the lamp and sight between the reed blade and the mouthpiece lower rails.

While holding the assembly in this position, squeeze the upper part of the stock with your thumb to check for a pocket warp (see page 24). The reed will spring away from the mouthpiece lower rails if the warp is present.

Dynamic Balancing

Rough Cutting With the Reed Knife and Clipboard

The clipboard offers secure handling of the reed during cutting operations and is constructed of a 1 1/4-inch-wide piece of 1/16-inch-thick clear plastic, cut to an appropriate length, and a 1 1/4-inch-wide stationery clip.[2]

The knife-cutting technique. For right-handers, place the tip of the left thumb just below the cutting area and use it as a brace for the knife. Butt the flat side of the knife blade against the thumb brace and cut the reed with a forward scraping motion.

Do not try to cut too long an area at any one thumb-brace position because the knife edge will flare away from the reed surface near the end of the stroke, resulting in incomplete cutting. Instead, divide the cutting area into smaller sections and cut them separately. Or slide the thumb brace along with the knife motion.

---

[2] *A larger clip with a wider jaw opening will be needed for baritone reeds.*

A medium-light cutting pressure should produce a powdered sawdust that confirms correct cutting technique. Heavier pressure, as evidenced by sawdust chunks and splinters, can gouge holes into the reed surface and needlessly dull the knife edge.

Illustration 7

ROUGH CUTTING THE REED BACK
WITH THE KNIFE AND CLIPBOARD

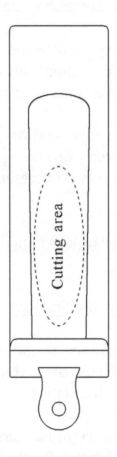

Cutting area

When cutting the back in this procedure, do not
allow the knife blade to touch the reed edges

Fine Finishing With Sandpaper and Surface Plate

This procedure requires a half-sheet of No. 400 wet-or-dry sandpaper[3] and a very flat surface upon which to work (such as, a kitchen cutting board or a section of drafting board). Coarser grades of sandpaper are not acceptable because they create too much friction heat. And friction heat can aggravate the very warp you are trying to control.

The sanding technique. If the warp is centered, as displayed by equal-width edge gaps, then the finger pressure on the reed shoulder should be as shown in Illustration 8a (see the following page). Or if the warp is offset, as displayed by one edge gap being wider than the other, then the finger pressure should be offset toward the wider gapped side as shown in Illustration 8b.

Give the reed 10 (or 20) down and up strokes, each about 1 inch long, bearing more heavily on the down strokes (the up strokes are only to reposition the reed for the next down stroke). Then check the reed with the desk lamp and mouthpiece.

This process can be repeated until the edge gaps barely disappear, but better results will be obtained by polish finishing on the flat mill file.

Polish Finishing on the Flat Mill File

The recommended tool for finishing reed backs is a flat mill file, single bastard cut, that is big enough to accommodate the largest size reeds upon which you intend to work. This file will flatten the reed without trapping friction heat and will produce a very smooth finish. The smooth finish will have a temporary gloss that is useful in analyzing the flatness of the reed back.

The cutting technique when using this tool is to place the file on the worktable and cut the reed in the same manner described for the sandpaper and surface plate.

---

[3] *Be sure that the sandpaper is unwrinkled and has no tendency to curl. Also, the sandpaper life can be extended if the sawdust is removed with a stiff-fiber brush.*

Illustration 8

CUTTING THE PRIMARY WARP

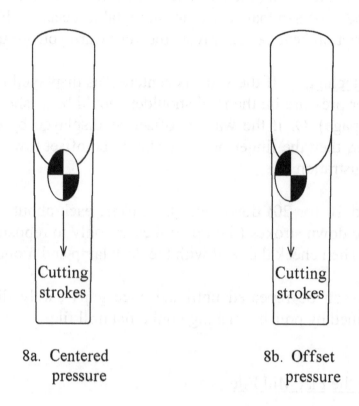

8a. Centered
pressure

8b. Offset
pressure

Modulation of the Concave and Primary Warps

Interdependency Between the Concave and Primary Warps

The primary warp has its interdependent partner in the concave warp, and the actions of these two warps are concentrated in moving the lower-area edges in opposite directions. That is, at the same time that the primary warp is trying, to move the edges away from the mouthpiece, the concave warp is trying to move them back toward the mouthpiece.

Prevailing Warps During the Static and Dynamic Shapes

The static shape. When the reed has been thoroughly rested, the concave warp will overpower the primary warp (there will be exceptions); and the reed edges will be held against the mouthpiece. This condition is termed the *Static Shape*.

Illustration 9

MODULATION OF THE CONCAVE AND PRIMARY WARPS

The first series represents a factory-cut reed
that has a flat back in its static shape

Reference _____ line

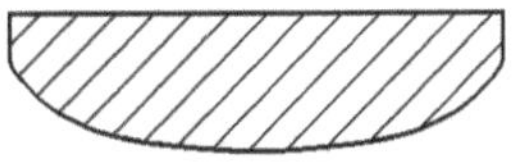

9a. Cross section,
Static shape:

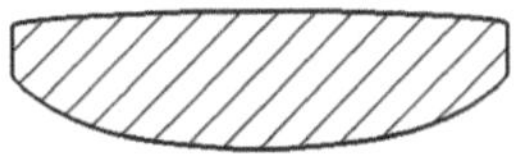

9b. Cross section,
Intermediate shape:

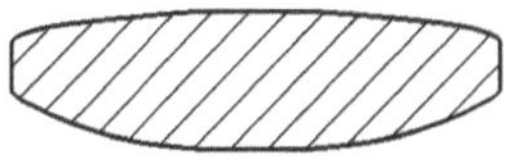

9c. Cross section,
Dynamic shape:

The concave and primary
warps are balanced at
this phase

As the primary warp begins
to take hold, moderate edge
gaps have been produced

Full development of the
primary warp has now
produced large edge gaps

The second series represents a partially balanced reed
that has a slightly concaved back in its static shape

Reference _____ line

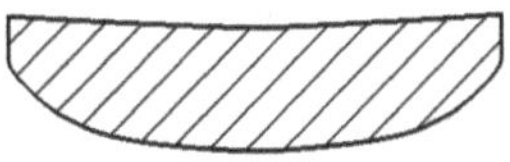

9d. Cross section,
Static shape:

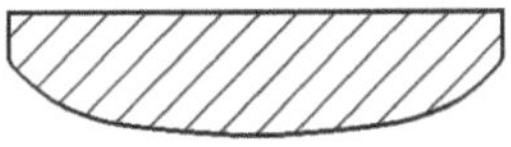

9e. Cross section,
Intermediate shape:

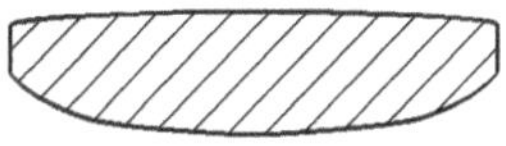

9f. Cross section,
Dynamic shape:

The concave warp is
overpowering the primary
warp

As the primary warp begins
to take hold, the forces are
now balanced

Full development of the
primary warp can now
produce only moderate
edge gaps

The third series represents a fully balanced reed that
has a deeply concaved back in its static shape

Reference _____ line

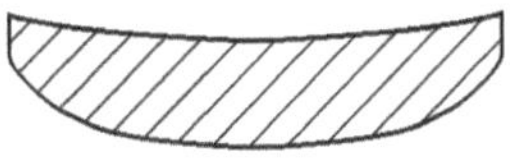

9g. Cross section,
Static shape:

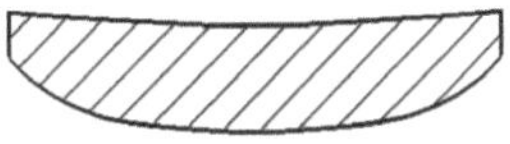

9h. Cross section,
Intermediate shape:

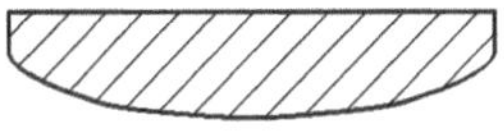

9i. Cross section,
Dynamic shape:

The concave warp is
overpowering the primary
warp

As the primary warp begins
to take hold, the concavity
is lessened

The flat back shows that
the concave and primary
warps are now balanced

Illustration 10

BACK VIEW: SEQUENTIAL SANDING/FILING AREAS
DURING THE CUTTING OF THE PRIMARY WARP

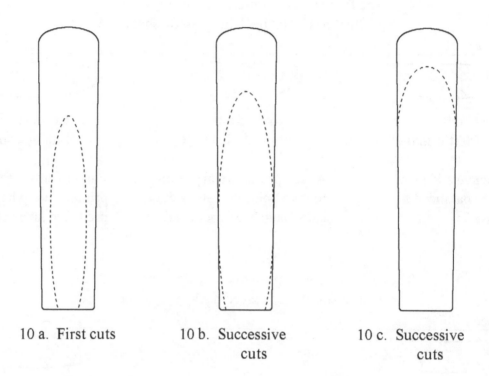

| 10 a. First cuts | 10 b. Successive cuts | 10 c. Successive cuts |

The dynamic shape. When the reed is placed into vibration, the primary warp will quickly overpower the concave warp; and the reed edges will be moved away from the mouthpiece. This condition is termed the *Dynamic Shape*.

How Dynamic Balancing Affects the Concave and Primary Warps

Each time the primary-warp bulge is recut, the center of mass is moved closer to the centerline of the cross section (because of the mass of wood removed from the flat side).

WHEN THIS HAPPENS, THE PROPORTIONAL FORCE OF

THE CONCAVE WARP IS INCREASED; AND THE PROPORTIONAL

FORCE OF THE PRIMARY WARP IS REDUCED.

This means that with repeated recuttings, the static shape will become deeply concaved; and the dynamic shape will become very flat, which results in the minimization of air leaks during the dynamic shape (review Illustration 9 on page 17).

The Effects of Weather and Moisture

Hot, dry weather (and dry winds) will amplify the powers of the primary and tangent warps, which often appear together in the dynamic shape. During dry summer heat (over 90 degrees) these two warps can become so extreme that the air leaks can only be lessened through recutting, not eliminated. Otherwise, the reed might be destroyed through the removal of too much wood.

In dealing with summer heat, it is recommended that the stocks of all reeds be thinned as explained on page 27, even if it is decided not to incorporate this feature during the milder seasons of the year.

Cold or damp weather will amplify the power of the concave warp, and less dynamic balancing will be needed.

Excess moisture in the reed can cause a permanent, leak-producing concave warp in the dynamic shape, sometimes through a delayed reaction. If it is a mild warp, it can be repaired; but if it is a severe warp, it cannot. This means that if a reed is intended to be played until water soaked or stored wetly on the mouthpiece, the primary warp should not be too deeply cut.

Also, intentional water soaking may have an advantage in combatting a primary warp, but the results are very undependable.

Classifications of Warps and Recommended Solutions

The four classifications of leak-producing warps are the *Primary Warp*, the *Tangent Warp*, the *Concave Warp*, and the *Pocket warp*.[4]

Remember that the primary and concave warps are interdependent between each other; but the tangent and pocket warps, if they appear at all, are individualities.

---

[4] *An arched stock (on page 125) is also a warp, but it does not produce an air leak.*

The Primary Warp

The primary warp is a natural occurrence that develops when the reed is set into vibration. Other promoters of the primary warp are wind, heat, dryness, and extreme aging.

In addition to the crosswise curving of the backside already discussed, the lengthwise shape of the warp will extend from the stock end nearly to the reed tip.

Illustration 11

CROSS SECTION: THE PRIMARY WARP II

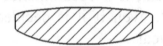

Symptoms. When the warp starts to appear, the pitch will begin to rise and the bite will become longer. As the warp becomes more severe, the highest and lowest notes will begin to cut out; and an audible bubbling or hissing of escaping air can develop, all combined with increased physical discomfort of the player.

Solution. As the reed is warmed up through playing, the backside is examined at 5-minute (or 10-minute) intervals. And when the edge gaps have developed enough to warrant cutting, the backside is reflattened as described on pages 14 through 17.

The Concave Warp

The concave warp is a backside tunnel that runs from the lower blade into the stock. This warp may be a natural occurrence, the result of cutting the backside, or both. The concave warp may be amplified by cold or damp weather or by too much water inside the reed.[5]

Illustration 12

CROSS SECTION: THE CONCAVE WARP

Symptoms. Since most dynamic-shaped concave warps will lie on the mouthpiece in a rocking chair-like fashion, air leaks can occur at the lower-blade edges, the stock edges, or through the stock end. And although a variety of problems may arise, most seem to include an insecure bite.

Solution. Mild dynamic-shaped concave warps may be reflattened on the sandpaper plate and/or flat file. But because this alteration of the cross section will also amplify the potential of the primary warp, the cutting should be no deeper than shown in Illustration 13b (see the following page).

After cutting to 13b depth, allow the reed to rest for several hours. Then play on the reed for exactly 10 minutes to see if the concavity has been eliminated. If not and the concave warp is still causing performance problems, completely reflatten the backside as shown in Illustration 14 (additional discussion of cutting the concave warp is presented on page 103; cutting a static-shaped concave warp is a separate topic presented on page 128).

---

[5] *Try this experiment to understand concave warps.*

Soak some concave-prone scrap reeds in a glass of water for several days. When they have become supersaturated, check the backsides. It will appear as though they (or some of them) are trying to curl back into the shape of the cane tubes from which they were cut.

Illustration 13

BACK VIEW: SEQUENTIAL CUTTING AREAS OF A MILD DYNAMIC-SHAPED CONCAVE WARP, PART 1

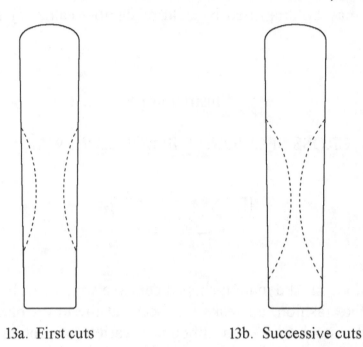

13a. First cuts   13b. Successive cuts

Illustration 14

BACK VIEW: SEQUENTIAL CUTTING AREAS OF A MILD DYNAMIC-SHAPED CONCAVE WARP, PART 2

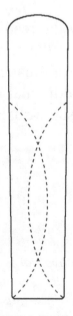

Optional final cuts

The Tangent Warp

The tangent warp is a natural occurrence wherein the reed curves outwardly from the mouthpiece rails (creating a tangent) without the supporting bulge of the primary warp. This warp is often found accompanying a primary warp in the dynamic shape, particularly during hot weather, at which time the tangent warp may be undetectable until the primary-warp bulge is removed.

Symptoms. The symptoms of the tangent warp are identical to those of the primary warp. Additionally, the tangent warp is likely to perform like a rocking chair on the mouthpiece bed.

Solution. The tangent warp may be sanded and filed in the same manner as the primary warp. However, since the crosswise section of the backside is already quite flat, the preliminary rough cutting with the reed knife is not practical.

Illustration 15

THE TANGENT WARP

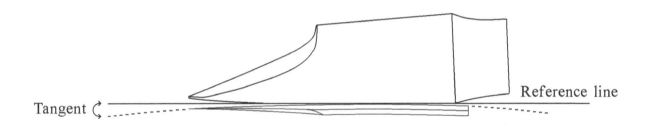

A tangent warp originating in the upper blade and extending toward the reed tip edge is not necessarily destructive to the reed performance and might even be an advantage in getting more air through the mouthpiece opening (see Resetting the Upper-Blade Angle on page 84). Oppositely, tangent warps originating in the lower blade or stock will always create a performance detriment, sometimes moderate, sometimes severe.

The Pocket Warp

The pocket warp is a backside hollow (pocket) in the upper part of the stock. And when the ligature is tightened, it will initiate a reflex action wherein the reed will spring away from the mouthpiece lower rails, thereby creating an air leak.

Illustration 16

THE POCKET WARP

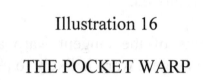

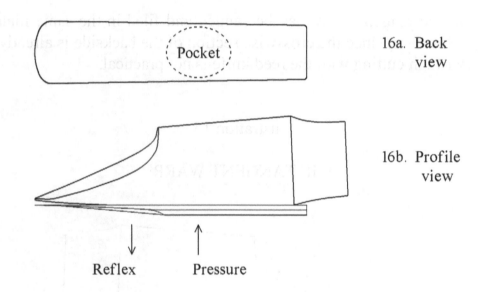

16a. Back view

16b. Profile view

Reflex   Pressure

Symptoms. This warp will usually not cause embouchure problems. Instead, the common symptom of a dynamic-shaped pocket warp is a severe weakening of the tone quality.

Solution 1. Although the pocket warp may be a natural occurrence, it can also be caused by cutting the back on the sandpaper plate. This is because some reeds will have very soft cane in the pocket area, and the sandpaper simply gouges too much wood from that area.

A different situation occurs, though, when reeds are polish finished on the flat mill file. The file will usually cut the reed without gouging the soft spot, and the pocket warp may therefore be prevented from occurring.

Solution 2. If a primary warp is also present, then the areas just above and below and extending slightly into the pocket area may be knifed as shown in Illustration 17 until the bulges have been removed, thereby blending the backside into the depression at a flatter angle.

Illustration 17

BACK VIEW: KNIFING A DYNAMIC-SHAPED POCKET WARP WHEN A PRIMARY WARP IS ALSO PRESENT

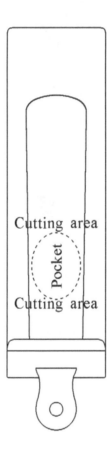

Solution 3. If the backside is flat or the player prefers not to use the knife, Illustration 18 on the next page shows how the reed may be sanded on the surface plate without placing finger pressure on the pocket area.

When applying either Solution 2 or 3, the reed should receive a final polish finishing on the flat mill file. Or the warp may be completely cut on the file.

Illustration 18

SANDING/FILING A DYNAMIC-SHAPED POCKET WARP

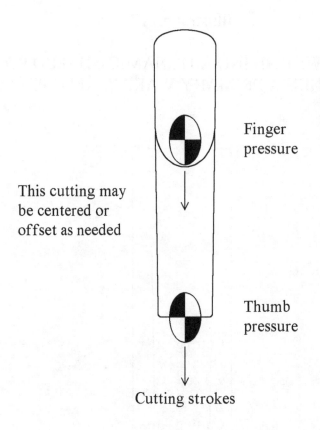

Finger pressure

This cutting may
be centered or
offset as needed

Thumb pressure

Cutting strokes

The two pressure points are applied simultaneously

❖   ❖   ❖

V. THINNING THE STOCK

This is an optional modification that will affect two aspects of the reed performance.[6] The first aspect is a reduction of the primary-warping potentials, which should quicken the break-in procedure. The second aspect is more complicated and concerns the resonance of the reed as discussed on page 32. And since some players may experience the resonance-reversal point (on page 35) rather quickly, these players may decide to decline this modification. Or they may apply it only to reeds that display a profound primary-warping tendency or to reeds comprised of unusually dense cane.

How the Primary Warp Is Affected

The cross section centerline and the center of mass can be brought even closer together by removing wood from the front side of the reed (see Illustration 19 on the following page). And since the full potential of the primary warp will be decreased, the break-in process should require fewer sessions. Also, this modification will preserve more lower-blade stiffness because less dynamic balancing will be needed, which means that ready-to-play-strength reeds will be less likely to require large clippings of their tips.[7]

When To Thin the Stock

Since this alteration will have a major influence on the warping actions, the stock should be thinned before the reed is placed into the break-in process.

---

[6] *A third aspect concerning the relative intonation of high F and low Bb is presented on page 123.*

[7] *The primary warp will nevertheless continue to develop and require the backside to be reflattened because the stock cross section will still be partially unbalanced while the lower-blade cross section will still be highly unbalanced.*

Illustration 19

COMPARING FRONT AND CROSS SECTION VIEWS
OF STANDARD AND THINNED STOCKS

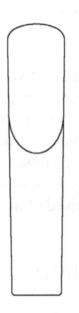

19b. Cross section:
Standard stock

19a. Front view:
Standard stock

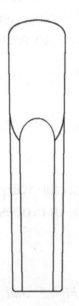

19d. Cross section:
Thinned stock

19c. Front view:
Thinned stock

Illustration 20

SLICING THE STOCK ON THE CUTTING JIG

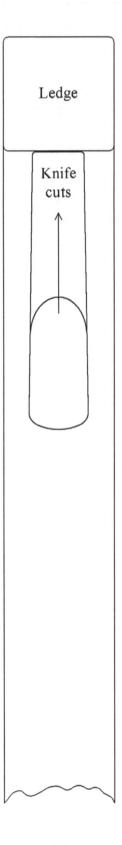

Some players, though, may prefer to delay this procedure until the tonal resonance and warping potential of the reed have been tested. And if a delayed cutting seems appropriate, it should still be performed very early in the playing life of the reed. Otherwise, too much wood may be removed from the backside of the stock during dynamic balancing; and the chance of developing a dynamic-shaped concave warp will be increased.

How To Thin the Stock

With the correct tools this modification can be quickly and safely performed in a two-stage operation. The first stage is to slice off some of the wood with a knife[8] while the reed is held in a cutting jig, and the second stage is to sandpaper the rough knife cuts to an even surface.

Slicing the Stock

The handheld cutting jig shown on page 29 is easily constructed from two pieces of wood (perhaps from a scrap of door molding) whereupon the ledge is glued to the base. The end-to-end length of the jig should be about 9 inches.

To slice the stock, fit the heel of the reed firmly against the ledge of the jig and hold it there with your thumb on the reed blade. Then place the knife edge near the reed shoulder and slice through the stock until the knife strikes the ledge. A few thin cutting strokes may be needed.

Sanding the Stock

The ragged knife cuts may be smoothed with a half-sheet of No. 220 wet-or-dry sandpaper used on the surface plate.[9] The appearance of the reed should be checked after each 30 or 40 cutting strokes, but check the reed more often as the work nears completion.

---

[8] *Do not use your best reed knife for this procedure because its edge might become chipped. Instead, use a thin-bladed steak knife or an inexpensive student-model reed knife.*

[9] *This piece of sandpaper will be difficult to use when it is brand-new because the reed will not slide over the surface. To break the surface, rub a scrap reed thoroughly across the sandpaper. Then carefully brush the paper to remove the sawdust.*

How Much Wood To Remove

A normally shaped stock should have nearly one-third of its thickness removed.[10]

The important thing to remember is that if too much wood is cut from the stock, the resonance may be aversely affected. And since even more wood will be cut from the stock backside during dynamic balancing, a margin of safety should be observed in the initial thinning.

Nevertheless, a removal of nearly one-third of the stock should be satisfactory for first experiments (assuming the stocks are of normal thickness when they leave the factory). And in some instances even more wood will be removed for fine adjustments later in the lives of the reeds.

The Shape of the Flattened Area

The crosswise surface must be parallel with the flat back of the reed.

The lengthwise surface may also be parallel with the flat back. But it is better to have a slight taper toward a thicker heel.

If an eccentricity in the cane-tube shape produces a surface that sharply tapers toward a thin heel, the thinning might be done entirely by sandpaper while sanding only the upper part of the stock. (A knife might split the stock, thus destroying the reed. Your choice, your risk.)

How the Reed Strength Is Affected

Because the hard wood at the stock edges will be left relatively intact, the weakening effect will be surprisingly small compared to the large mass of wood that is removed.

---

[10] *It is not necessary to cut the shoulder to an exact micrometer thickness. But if a measurement for the upper flattened area (just within the rainbow-shaped tip of the cut area) is discovered that seems generally correct, then applying the measurement is definitely recommended. (As a suggestion, .095 inch has proved to be acceptable for medium-density alto and tenor reeds.)*

How the Pivot-Point Location Is Affected

When the left and right sides of the upper flattened area are the same thickness, the pivot point should gravitate toward the top of the rainbow-shaped tip of the thinned area at the exact crosswise center of the reed.

One problem may occur, though, if the stock was initially too thick; and thinning it resulted in very narrow bands of bark remaining along the stock edges. The nearly rectangular stock produced in this situation might cause the pivot point to drift away from the center of the rainbow tip.

To correct this condition, the edges of the stock just below the shoulder must be rounded with a file. When performing this filing, the front and profile views must be frequently checked for exact matching of these edge areas. Additionally, for sake of appearance the rounding of the edges can continue for the entire length of the stock.

How the Resonance Is Affected

Free Vibrations

If you listen closely through the neck of the saxophone, a faint, rustling tone will be heard in the air column of the instrument (just as the "ocean" can be heard when a conch shell is held to the ear). The internal vibrations causing this tone are called free vibrations,[11] and in wind-instrument bores, free vibrations are characterized by a sustained tone that is created without a deliberate power source.[12]

Listen long enough, and you will find that external sounds will amplify the volume of the rustling tone. And no matter what general pitch the external sound may have, the pitch of the rustling tone will correspond to whatever note is being keyed on the instrument by the player.

---

[11] *They are called free vibrations because being unrestrained, they are free to vibrate according to their nature.*

[12] *The friction noise of air circulating throughout the room is sufficient to bring the rustling tone within the threshold of audibility.*

The amplification of the rustling tone is created because some of the external-sound overtones will be vibrating at the same frequencies as those already present in the free vibrations of the instrument. When this happens, part of the energy from the external overtones will be used to intensify the matching vibrations of the air column. This intensification or sympathetic vibration is termed a state of *Resonance*.

In their natural state, as just described, the free vibrations are so weak that they can barely be considered an audible tone. When a vibrating reed is placed in direct contact with the air column, however, this condition will be dramatically changed.

Forced Vibrations

The crowing of the reed on the mouthpiece is called a forced vibration because it requires the application of a deliberate power source (the player's breath).

The squawking of the crowed reed produces irregular vibrations (small gaps of silence can be observed even though the breath pressure is constant), and the sound is so harsh that it can barely be considered a musical tone. When the instrument air column is placed in direct contact with the beating reed, however, these conditions will also be dramatically changed.

The Interaction of Free Vibrations and Forced Vibrations

The function of the forced vibrations is to amplify the volume of the free vibrations into a full, audible sound. And as the player's breath pressure is decreased or increased, the dynamic range of the instrument will be established, perhaps from pp to fff.

When the strength of the free vibrations has been amplified, the free vibrations will in turn produce two striking effects on the crowed reed.

The first effect is to smooth the harsh and irregular vibrations of the crowed reed into a true musical tone.

The second effect is to align vibration frequencies of the reed to match those of the air column itself, thus establishing the tonal range of the instrument from low Bb to high F.[13]

Mutual resonance. As long as the reed is kept vibrating, the reed and air column will exist in a state of mutual resonance throughout the fundamental tone and overtones of the sound. That is, the air column will vibrate in sympathy with the reed; and the reed will vibrate in sympathy with the air column.

Actually, most reeds will do an acceptable job of resonating throughout the dynamic and tonal ranges of the instrument (after all, that is what they are designed to do). But since the purpose of adjustments is an attempt to allow ordinary reeds to become great reeds, the causes of slow-responding, stiff-playing reeds must be sought. And the causes will often be that the reeds are comprised of cane that is too dense or that the damping effect of the excess wood is too great, both of which will limit the resonating qualities of the reeds.

The Damping Effect

Part of the player's breath energy will be uselessly absorbed by the wood of the reed. This absorption is called a *damping effect*.

---

[13] *This effect may be examined by experiment:*

First, take the instrument and play a sustained middle C (third space in the treble clef). While holding this tone, begin to lip the note downward to find the lowest note that can be produced before the tone cuts out. With ordinary luck you may be able to lip the note down about a minor third before the reed stops vibrating. Next, simply depress the keys to finger a low C and observe how easily and strongly the note may be blown.

What happens is that the free vibrations will change their vibrating frequency whenever the length of the air column is manipulated by the keys. And the free vibrations will then adjust the vibrating frequency of the reed in sympathy with that of their own new frequency.

And the reason why middle C cannot be lipped down an entire octave to low C is because the embouchure and oral cavity adjustments will have insufficient effect on the frequency rate of the free vibrations.

Finally, a compromise is always made. The reed will raise the pitch of the air column, and the air column will lower the pitch of the reed. An intermediate of the two forces is the pitch that is produced.

Obviously, since reeds are comprised of damping material, the damping effect will always be expressed. But when excess wood is present, it will absorb energy that could be better used for vibrating the reed and air column. And the extra damping will be even more detrimental if the reed is made of cane that is too dense.[14]

Removing excess damping. Although some extra wood will be removed as the blade and backside are brought into balance, a reed may still contain useless material that will contribute to a characteristic "dead" tone.

For even more damping removal, many people will find that the front-side wood of the stock serves no useful purpose. When the stock is thinned as detailed in this section, the excess damping will be removed; and a pleasant ringing will develop in the tone. As a consequence, the reed should be much easier to play.[15]

The Resonance-Reversal Point

If too much wood is removed from the front side of the stock, the reed may begin to lose its resonance. This is because the fundamental tone of the forced vibrations will be moving out of alignment with that of the free vibrations as the needed wood is removed. And this might be interpreted as a loss of center in the tone.

Restoring lost resonance. If the lost resonance is very slight, it might be restored by clipping the reed tip. In this situation an advantage will be found if the thinned stock has a mild taper toward a thicker heel. Then the clipping will produce a slightly thicker shoulder that will contribute to the now-needed extra damping. This solution will work, though, only if the lost resonance is just barely noticeable.

---

[14] *The opposite effect may be found in reeds comprised of cane that is not dense enough; that is, the tone may be too resonant or too bright.*

These reeds may also benefit from thinning their stocks for the purpose of reducing their primary-warping potentials. And to add the needed extra damping, their blades may be left with slightly thicker cuts. Then the extra wood and the water it contains should produce mellower tone qualities.

[15] *Sawing off the end of the stock will not work. This is because being so far displaced from the active part of the reed, the end of the stock has very little (if any) effect in the vibrating and damping actions.*

Why the Thinning Procedure May Be Declined

Because of wide variations in mouthpiece designs and blowing styles, it is apparent that some players may reach the resonance-reversal point upon the initial thinning of the stock. Or the point may be so closely approached that additional cutting of the reed will endanger its performance. Therefore, if experiments prove that this modification is incompatible with your playing style, this alteration may be declined.

Conclusions

If this procedure is complementary to your playing style, thinning the stock is a quick-and-easy way of improving performance and shortening the break-in process with little chance of damaging the reed (although some experience will be needed to develop your conception of a properly shaped stock).

Also, if the clamping action of the ligature is affected, a smaller diameter ligature that is capable of holding the reed by its edges might be needed.

It is also suggested that if this modification is not complementary to your playing style or if you do not wish to change ligatures, the stock should be thoroughly filed and balanced, being aware of problems such as those presented on pages 2 and 3.

Finally, observe that the stock does not necessarily need to be sliced with a knife. Instead, the vertical center section of the stock may be filed until the bark disappears. This part-way adaptation may offer a moderate improvement in the warping and resonating aspects of the reed.

❖   ❖   ❖

VI. PREVIEW OF CUTTING THE BLADE

The Empirical and Micrometer Methods Explained

The Empirical Method

For the purposes of this book, the empirical method of adjusting reeds will include any techniques or tools used to evaluate the aspects of a reed with one exclusion. The exclusion is that the micrometer and gridwork are not used to reproduce ideal thickness measurements derived from other successful reeds (the probable reasons for this exclusion are that the player has not had the opportunity to assemble the tool or that the ideal measurements have not yet been discovered).

The techniques may include visual tests, blowing tests, and bending tests. Additional tools, such as, model reeds, calipers, a magnifying glass, a ruler, and so forth, will all be considered part of the empirical method.

One exception to the rule may be found when dealing with a reed of unusual strength, density, or thickness. When this type of reed is encountered, the micrometer assembly may be used to match the left and right sides of the reed. But since the ideal measurements will not be applied, the micrometer will be used as an empirical tool in this situation.

The Micrometer Method

This method of adjusting reeds uses the micrometer and gridwork to duplicate the ideal thickness measurements derived from other successful reeds.

Generally, the upper blades of all reeds will be cut to the same, predetermined thicknesses (allowing for slight variations, such as, when the factory creates an area that is too thin). Additionally, precise lengthwise curves for the lower blade may be calculated for each individual reed; and these curves may also be applied by using the micrometer.

The easiest way to use the micrometer method is to cut a reed to the ideal measurements first. Then the empirical method may be used for fine adjustments.

Blade-Cutting Tools

The Reed Knife

The reed knife should be a professional model featuring a hardened-steel, V-shaped blade. Be sure to get a hollow-ground blade because it will be much easier to sharpen than a flat-sided blade (nonetheless, honing the blade the very first time can be a major project).

The Bench Stone

A combination medium-/fine-grit stone (about 6 inches long by 2 inches wide) will be satisfactory. Be sure to get a high-quality stone because the surface of an inexpensive stone will crumble and destroy the straight cutting edge of the knife.

Honing the Knife Edge

First, improvise some type of stop or board with which to mount the stone so it will not slide off the worktable into your lap.

Fit the stone in a lengthwise position against the stop with the medium-grit side up and an absorbent rag beneath the stone. Then cover the surface of the stone with cutting oil (or whatever else is available—never use a dry stone because it will become permanently clogged with metal dust).

Hold the knife with both hands and give one side of the blade 100 down-and-up strokes to make the edge perfectly straight. Then turn the knife around and give the other side of the blade a matching 100 down-and-up strokes. Keep repeating this procedure until each side of the blade has received 300 strokes.

Next, continue the process using the fine-grit side of the stone until each side of the blade has received 200 more cutting strokes The total number of cutting strokes will be 1,000 (500 strokes on each side of the blade).

Finally, examine the blade edge for feathering (bending and rippling) and work any problem areas on the fine-grit stone until the blade edge is a perfect V shape. Then wash the stone in soap and water.

Needle Files

These files are about 6 inches long and are made in a variety of shapes. The types best suited for reed working should present a flat, narrow surface to the reed.

The pattern of the teeth. The teeth of the files should be criss-crossed because this allows better directional control of the cutting strokes, and you will need at least two files with different tooth patterns for separate cutting conditions. One file should have wide-spaced teeth for working on new reeds or harder wood, and the other should have narrow-spaced teeth for working on well-used reeds or softer wood.

The cutting technique. The files may be used to cut the blade (on or off the clipboard) in any direction that seems appropriate, including back against the grain. But if back-grain cutting is to be applied near the reed tip, be sure to use the narrow-toothed file and be careful not to snag the tip fibers.

The limitations of files. Although these files will produce very smooth surfaces, they are not as well-suited for micrometer work as a reed knife.

Also, it is sometimes difficult to control the cutting when working on the reed tip and outline of the upper reed heart. When working on these areas, the file may need to be supplemented with an alternate cutting tool.

Rush

The exterior ribbing of these wood-like tubes is an excellent abrasive for cutting reeds, and a piece of rush is very easy to use.

The packaged pieces available in music stores are about the right length (perhaps 1 1/2 inches to 2 1/2 inches long), but the round tubes must be pressed flat before being used.

Flattening the rush. Place a couple of pieces of water-soaked rush beneath a very large, heavy book on the worktable. Then keep adding weight to the top of the book until the rush is crushed absolutely flat. After about a day and a half of being pressed, the rush will have dried into permanently flat pieces.

Or even better, the water-soaked rush may be dried between two blocks of wood while being pressed flat in the jaws of a bench vise.

The cutting technique. Lay the reed on a flat surface (do not use the surface plate if it is made of wood or plastic) and place the rush ribs crosswise over the area to be cut. The rush will then work like a flexible file when it is rubbed over the reed under the direct pressure of one fingertip.

Sandpaper Strips

These may be scissored from sheets of No. 400 or No. 600 wet-or-dry sandpaper. To ensure that only very small areas of the reed will be cut (and that adjacent areas will not be cut), the strips should be quite narrow.

Identification Numbers

Working with only one reed at a time is not a practical way to produce a supply of performance-ready reeds. Instead, two to four reeds for your principal instrument may be simultaneously involved in the break-in process (and a few more reeds may be in the working supply if you prefer to rotate their performance use).

To ensure that the unique qualities of these reeds will be well-remembered, each reed will receive an identification number; and a matching-numbered abstract (information sheet) will also be prepared for each reed.

Where To Place the Number

The front side of the stock is the best place for the identification number.[16]

---

[16] *If a temporary number is to be marked on a thinned stock, the number should be lightly written to prevent the pencil point from scarring the soft wood. A permanent number should be darkly written on the thinned stock. Pencil writing directly on the bark will be more durable if the bark surface is first roughened with a piece of coarse sandpaper.*

Temporary Numbers

A temporary number may be marked when the reed is placed into the break-in process.

Two important features of an identification-number system are: (1) the number should reflect the month in which the reed enters the break-in process (the month may change before the reed is placed into performance, which might also involve a seasonal weather change that can affect the reed); and (2) the reeds produced within that month should be sequentially numbered to establish their individualities at a glance.

Permanent Numbers

The temporary number may be changed to a permanent number when the reed is placed into performance, and the permanent number should also reflect the month and sequence in which the reed is brought into the working supply.

Also, there may be enough room on the stock for additional journalizing. This information may be a cryptic abbreviation of a band name, the place of first performance, or some quality of the reed to be emphasized—anything at all to help establish the identity, history, or quality of the reed at a glance.

Illustration 21

A PERMANENT IDENTIFICATION NUMBER

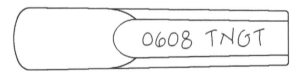

<u>Legend</u>

06 = Month of June
08 = Reed No. 8
TNGT = Problem tangent warp

Abstracts

An abstract is a sheet of paper upon which the details of a reed are journalized. An abstract may be designed for either the empirical method or the micrometer method.

Empirical Abstracts

A convenient form for an empirical abstract is to draw a picture of the reed in the center of the paper, and appropriate comments may be detailed in the wide margins as shown in Illustration 22.

Illustration 22

AN EMPIRICAL ABSTRACT

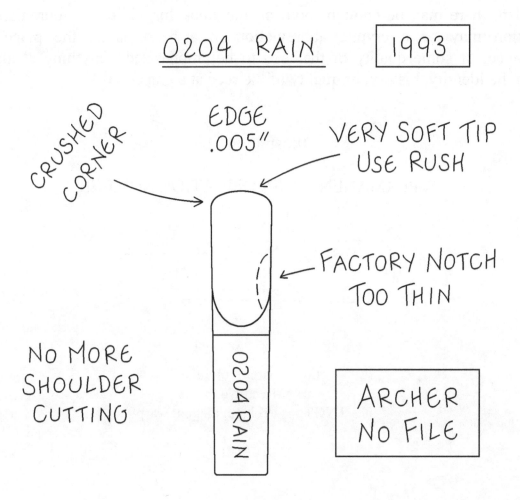

Micrometer Abstracts

The purpose of a micrometer abstract is to record the thickness measurements of a reed at the corresponding intersections of the gridwork. This system will allow the player to visualize the curves and thicknesses of the reed blade at a glance.

Simplified micrometer measurements. The standard written forms of micrometer measurements are confusing to read, so the simplified-measurement system shown in Table 1 will be used for the micrometer abstracts. Within this system whole thousandths of an inch are reduced to their basic number (e.g., .006 inch will be simply stated as 6). And a half-thousandth of an inch will be shown as a + symbol (e.g., .0095 inch will be simply stated as 9+).

Table 1

THE SIMPLIFIED-MICROMETER-MEASUREMENT SYSYEM

Number-and- Word Form	Decimal-Number- and-Symbol Form	Simplified Form
6 thousandths of an inch	.006"	6
9 1/2 thousandths of an inch	.0095"	9+
13 1/2 thousandths of an inch	.0135"	13+
18 thousandths of an inch	.018"	18
23 thousandths of an inch	.023"	23
28 thousandths of an inch	.028"	28

The lengthwise measurement lines. These lines are shown in Illustration 23. The lines are spaced 3 millimeters apart and begin 3 millimeters below the absolute tip edge. The edge lines and centerline (at 6, 0, and 6 millimeters) extend downwardly for the full length of the blade, or as close to the shoulder as can be measured in 3-millimeter increments. But the quarter lines (at 3 and 3 millimeters) extend downwardly only to the micrometer-method bite line at 15 millimeters (plotting curves for the lower-blade quarter lines is optional).

Illustration 23

THE LENGTHWISE MEASUREMENT LINES

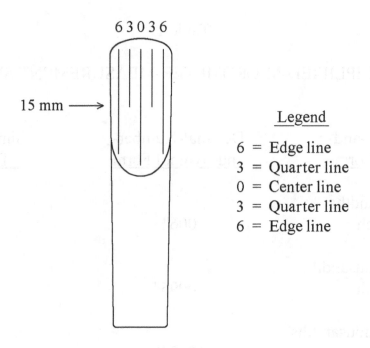

Legend

6 = Edge line
3 = Quarter line
0 = Center line
3 = Quarter line
6 = Edge line

The ideal measurements. Because of variations in reed strengths, mouthpieces, and blowing styles each player will have to experiment to find the ideal measurements for the upper blade.[17] When the ideal measurements have been found, the ideal measurements will be written on the micrometer abstract, not the actual measurements of the reed upper blade.

---

[17] *Easy methods of developing ideal measurements and lengthwise curves are shown in the appendix.*

The lower blade will be similarly treated. That is, the curves from the bite line to the shoulder will be mathematically calculated for each reed. And the calculated measurements will be written on the abstract, not the actual measurements of the reed lower blade.

Applying the measuring/cutting procedure. The reed blade will be measured on the gridwork as shown below. When a reed area is discovered that is thicker than the corresponding abstract measurement, a pencil mark will be made on the reed. Then the area (or areas) will be cut on the clipboard to the abstract specification.

Illustration 24

MEASURING THE BLADE THICKNESS
ON THE 3-MILLIMETER-SQUARE GRIDWORK

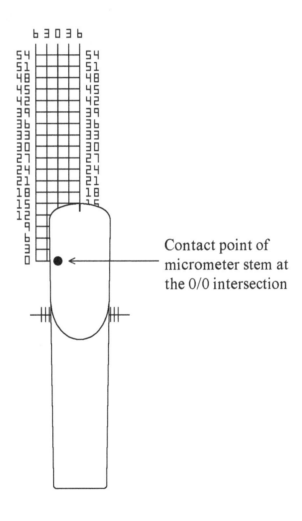

Contact point of micrometer stem at the 0/0 intersection

The witness mark at the center of the reed
tip is positioned at the 6/15 intersection

45

Table 2

A COMPLETE MICROMETER ABSTRACT FOR A TENOR SAX REED

	6	3	0	3	6
3	6	6+	6+	6+	6
6	9+	11	11+	11	9+
9	13+	16	17	16	13+
12	18	21+	23	21+	18
15	23	28	30	28	23
		(7)	(8)	(7)	
18	28		38		28
	(6)		9		(6)
21	34		47		34
	7		10		7
24	41		57		41
	8		11		8
27	49		68		49
	10		12		10
30	59		80		59
	13		14		13
33	72		94		72
			16		
36			110		
Grid line	Left edge line	Left quarter line	Center-line	Right quarter line	Right edge line

The gridwork numbers (the numbers outside the bracket) represent the measurement increments in 3-millimeter squares, and the micrometer measurements (the numbers inside the bracket) are simplified in thousandths of an inch

Table 3

A SIMPLIFIED MICROMETER ABSTRACT FOR A TENOR SAX REED

Grid line	Both edge lines	Both quarter lines	Center-line
3	6	6+	6+
6	9+	11	11+
9	13+	16	17
12	18	21+	23
15	23	28	30
		(7)	(8)
18	28		38
	(6)		9
21	34		47
	7		10
24	41		57
	8		11
27	49		68
	10		12
30	59		80
	13		14
33	72		94
			16
36			110

The right-side quarter-line and edge-line columns in Table 2 have been eliminated to avoid needless duplication of the left-side columns, the upper gridwork markings (6, 3, 0, 3, 6) have been eliminated because they are so easily remembered, and the bracket has been eliminated because it is unnecessary

47

Complete abstracts. A complete abstract for a tenor sax reed is shown in Table 2 on page 46, and this abstract is comprised of two parts. The first part is a large, two-line bracket surrounded by the gridwork measurement numbers while the second part contained within the bracket shows the micrometer measurements in simplified form.

The upper-blade measurements in this abstract represent the ideal thickness curves for a hypothetical player (remember that your ideal measurements will be slightly different). And since these same measurements will be repeated for every reed and abstract, the measurements and curves will be known to be correct; so no other upper-blade calculations will be needed at this time.

Because of variations in the lower-blade shaping from reed to reed, the lower-blade curves will be calculated directly on the abstract; and this is the reason for the inbetween numbers shown in the lower-blade sections of the abstracts.

In viewing Table 2, however, one great redundancy can be observed. This redundancy is the needless duplication of the left-side and right-side edge lines and quarter lines.

Simplified abstracts. Because the micrometer measurements of a reed are ideally identical between its left and right sides, having to maintain two sets of identical numbers on the abstract is unnecessary. The measurement columns on the left side of the abstract can represent both sides of the reed as shown in Table 3 on page 47.

Also, the crosswise gridwork numbers (at 6, 3, and 0 millimeters) are so easily remembered that they can be completely eliminated (along with the bracket).

When an abstract has been simplified in this manner, it will be much easier to read and maintain than a complete abstract. This will also allow the measurement columns to be spread out across the paper, which will leave more room for writing other details.

Coding the micrometer abstract for imaginary measurements. Although the simplified abstract will display the perfect measurements for a reed, the physical measurements of the reed may differ in some areas. So a method of recording these differences on the abstract will enable the player to visualize the actual reed shaping at a glance.

The variations of the reed thicknesses can be quickly marked and read by using code symbols on the abstract. The symbols will be a – sign (minus sign) to mark an area that is 1/2 thousandth to 1 thousandth of an inch too thin, a = sign (double minus

Table 4

CODING THE MICROMETER ABSTRACT
FOR IMAGINARY MEASUREMENTS

3	– 6	6+	6+
6	9+	11	11+
9	13+	16 –	– 17 –
12	18 –	– 21+ –	= 23 =
15	– 23 –	– 28 –	= 30 =
		(7)	(8)
18	– 28 =		= 38 =
	(6)		9
21	34 =		– 47 –
	7		10
24	41 =		– 57 –
	8		11
27	49 =		– 68 –

Code Signs

– The minus signs represent areas that are 1/2 thousandth to 1 thousandth of an inch too thin;

= The double minus signs represent areas that are more than 1 thousandth of an inch too thin; and

+ Any plus signs (not shown) will represent areas that are at least 1/2 thousandth of an inch too thick

Sign Placement

Signs placed at the left side of a column represent the left side of the reed;

Signs placed at the right side of a column represent the right side of the reed; and

Since the center of the reed has no left or right side, the signs are placed on both sides of the column for better visibility

sign) to mark an area that is more than 1 thousandth of an inch too thin, and a + sign (plus sign) to mark an area that is at least 1/2 thousandth of an inch too thick.

The code symbols will be placed adjacently to the corresponding abstract measurements. If a symbol is to represent the left side of the reed, the symbol will be placed at the left side of the measurement column. Or if a symbol is to represent the right side of the reed, the symbol will be placed at the right side of the measurement column. The centerline of the reed, though, has no left or right side. So the centerline codings will be placed on both sides of the measurement column for better visibility.

Generally, the ideal measurements will show the maximum thicknesses that should be allowed. And since the thick areas of the reed will be corrected with the cutting tools, the + symbols will be rarely used (they might be used, however, for a temporary experiment). Also, if a reed has only a few areas that are slightly thin, then the performance of the reed may not be noticeably affected; and the use of the − signs might be disregarded. However, if the reed has many thin areas, which is the usual case, then the abstract should be thoroughly coded with − and = signs.

Table 4 on the preceding page shows a typical application of this system. When viewing this abstract, the player will already know that the measurement numbers are correct; and attention will be immediately drawn to the abundance of = signs. The player will quickly see that the lower right edge has been deeply notched by the factory and that the sanding of the primary warp is intruding into the upper blade.

<u>Coding the abstract for intentional variations</u>. The coding for imaginary measurements just discussed concerns areas of the reed that are accidentally different than the ideal measurements. But there will be other times when variations from the ideal measurements will be intentional.

The intentional variations are usually designed to compensate for slight problems in the cane density, such as, designing a resistance section to compensate for soft cane in the upper blade or extra thinning of the reed tip to compensate for hard cane in that area.

Therefore, another code may be used on the abstract for intentional variations. This code is to write the variation measurement number on the abstract instead of the ideal measurement number and to draw a circle around the number to note its significance (see Table 5 on page 55).

Difficulties in Measuring the Blade

The micrometer is a sensitive instrument and the reed is a flexible object, so the following problems will frequently be found.

Calibrating the Micrometer

The micrometer stem is a spring-loaded mechanism that can dent the paper upon which the gridwork is printed (it will also dent plastic or soft metal if the gridwork is etched on them). To prevent the dented area from affecting the thickness measurements, the micrometer must be calibrated before each use.

To calibrate the micrometer, a flat, metal feeler gauge (the type used to adjust automobile ignition points) measuring .005 inch is slipped between the surface of the gridwork and the micrometer stem. The adjustable face of the micrometer is then turned until the dial arm points directly at .005 inch.

Heat Sensitivity of the Micrometer Assembly

If your micrometer assembly is sensitive to body heat and breath heat, it may become uncalibrated because of a temperature change. So the calibration must be rechecked while the tool is in use.

Alignment of the Reed on the Gridwork

Factory-cut reeds are wider at the tip than at the heel. Although it might appear that the edge of the reed should be parallel with the lengthwise gridwork line, this will result in a skewed edge line. Instead, be sure that the reed is always held in a straight position on the gridwork; especially, when measuring the lower-blade edges.

Holding the Reed Flat on the Gridwork

Used reeds will display a lengthwise bowing around the mouthpiece-facing area that will prevent the reed from lying flat on the gridwork. The spring tension of the micrometer stem will press the reed into a flatter shape, but the reed may still be slightly bowed and producing a false measurement reading. To correct this effect, finger pressure must be used on the reed just in front of the micrometer stem.

51

Another effect will be observed when the primary warp is present in the reed. This effect is a side-to-side rocking action that can change the measurement readings; particularly, those of the edge lines. To correct this effect, the finger pressure in front of the micrometer stem must be angled toward the edge of the reed.

Quick-Concaving Reeds

An occasional reed will begin to regain its static shape within a few minutes of being removed from the mouthpiece for checking. When this happens, the backside will become quickly concaved; and the centerline measurements for the lower blade will be seriously distorted. To correct this effect, the reed must be played for another few minutes to flatten the concave warp. Then the area may be accurately measured (be sure to write "quick concave" on the abstracts for these reeds).

The Viewing Angle

It is undesirable to crane your neck over the reed to ensure its alignment at a gridwork intersection because your head will have to be pulled back to read the dial gauge. When this maneuvering is repeated for many measurements, the procedure can become quite uncomfortable. Instead, hold your head in front of the dial gauge so that the gridwork lines can also be easily seen. Then make as many measurements from this position as possible.

When working with the extra length of a baritone reed (or possibly a tenor reed), it will be necessary to peer over the gauge to align the lower-blade measurement positions. So try to find a comfortable and consistent head motion for working in this area.

Difficulties in Cutting the Blade

Reed cane is an inconsistent material with which to work, so an extra-careful cutting of a brand-new reed will prevent the accidental removal of too much wood.

The general rule for cutting medium-density cane is that 10 medium-light strokes of the knife will remove 1 thousandth of an inch of wood from a small, average area of the blade. But because of inconsistencies in cane textures and varying states of water absorption (water will soften the cane), this rule must be viewed with suspicion until the cutting resistance of the reed has been tested during the first break-in session.

How the Blade Curvature Affects the Depth of the Cutting Strokes

The lengthwise direction of the grain will be nearly parallel with the flat back of the reed, but the front side of the blade will have a gradually increasing curve toward the reed shoulder.

Illustration 25

CROSS SECTION PROFILE: THE DIRECTION OF THE GRAIN

The grain lies nearly parallel with the flat
back of the reed, not the curved front

This means that as the cutting progresses from the tip to the shoulder, the knife will be working at a more severe angle across the shear of the grain. And as the angle becomes more severe, the wood will present greater resistance to the knife.

The upper edges. The curve in this area lies nearly parallel with the flat backside, and the wood may offer the least resistance to the knife cuts. Often only 2 to 4 strokes of the knife will remove 1 thousandth of an inch; particularly, if the interior of the cane is quite wet (remember, the reed must be thoroughly dried by the fingers before measuring and cutting—this will dry the surface grains but not the interior grains).

The bite-line edges. As the cutting approaches the bite-line edges, the resistance may increase as though a hard spot has been discovered. This may indeed be a hard spot, but the usual cause is the increased angle at which the knife is crossing the grain. Around this area 5 or more cutting strokes may remove 1 thousandth of an inch.

The lower-blade edges. This area presents the most severe angle for the knife to cross the grain, and the wood is often naturally harder because it was grown close to the bark (review page 1). The common course is to assume that 10 cuts will remove 1 thousandth of an inch of wood. But when checking the progress with the micrometer, it may be found that only 1/2 thousandth has been removed. So the cutting may be repeated until the measurement is correct.

Some reeds will contain very tough wood in the lower edges and may also be 5 or more thousandths of an inch too thick. When this situation is discovered, it is best to do some rough cutting with a file rather than wear out the knife edge on the hard wood. Then remeasure the area and resume cutting with the knife.

Coding the Abstract for Cutting Strokes

When a brand-new reed is being cut, its resistance to the knife will be unknown. For safe cutting always assume that the upper edges will need only 2 or 3 cutting strokes to remove 1 thousandth of an inch of wood. When this cutting is applied and the area remeasured, an estimate of the exact number of strokes needed to remove 1 thousandth of an inch can be made. The estimated number can then be coded on the abstract adjacently to the corresponding ideal-measurement number.

The cutting-stroke code is to write the number of strokes followed by an equal sign (i.e., 3 =, 4 =, 5 =, etc.). And to ensure that the equal signs are not mistaken for the double minus signs used to mark thin areas, the stroke number and equal sign will be placed in a small box as shown in Table 5.

When the upper-edge section of the abstract has been coded in this manner, subsequent adjustments of the areas should be easier to apply with less risk of removing too much wood. But try to keep the number of codings to a minimum. Otherwise, the abstract may become too cluttered with markings.

Working With Very Soft Cane

If the cane of a particular reed is too soft and you do not wish to change to the fine-tooth file, then an alternate method of knife cutting may be used. Instead of coding the abstract for cutting strokes, the reed is allowed to dry out for a few minutes before adjusting (write "dry out" or "soft wood" near the upper-edge section of the abstract). Then the drier wood will offer greater resistance to cutting as displayed by a brittle feeling when it is scraped by the knife. Just be sure to cut the reed tip before it begins to wrinkle and check for a slight concave warp before measuring the lower blade.

Table 5

A FULLY CODED MICROMETER ABSTRACT
FOR A TENOR SAX REED

3		− 6		⑥	⑥
6	[4 =]	9+	[3 =]	11	11+
9		13+	↓	16 −	− 17 −
12	↓	18 −		− 21+ −	= 23 =
15	[2 =]	− 23 −		− 28 −	= 30 =
				(7)	(8)
18	↓	− 28 =			= 38 =
		(6)			9
21		34 =			− 47 −
		7			10
24		41 =			− 57 −
		8			11
27		49 =			− 68 −
		10			12
30		59			80
		13			
33		72			

Observations

The reed tip has been thinned an extra 1/2 thousandth of an inch to compensate for hard wood in that area, and the intentional variations have been circled to note their significance;

The centerline (the rightmost column) is shorter than the edge lines because the stock has been thinned; and

A soft spot was discovered at the left-edge bite line

Controlled Cutting

Knife Speed

The reed must not be attacked with a flurry of fast knife strokes. Instead, a deliberate, medium-tempo speed must be applied so the texture of the cane can be felt through the knife and the development of sawdust can be closely observed.

The Length and Depth of the Cuts

The length. When a section of a lengthwise measurement line has been marked into 3-millimeter-long cutting areas, the cutting strokes will be either 3 millimeters or 6 millimeters long from any thumb-brace position (review page 13). To produce the most even surface, the cuts should extend to 6 millimeters wherever it is practical to do so.

Rough-cutting depth. If an area of the reed is a few thousandths of an inch too thick (this often happens in the lower blade of a brand-new reed), a maximum of 2 thousandths may be removed before remeasuring the area.

Fine-cutting depth. As the finishing cuts are made to the reed, they must be no deeper than 1 thousandth of an inch; especially, in the upper blade. This will also produce the most even surface.

How To Resolve Gouges

Even when the knife speed and cutting depth are being controlled, the knife may wobble or an unexpected soft spot may be discovered, both of which can create a small gouge. When this happens, the remaining cutting strokes must be angled diagonally toward the edge of the reed. Then only the high spots will be cut, and the gouge will not be enlarged (or the needle file might be used to flatten the area).

Overlapping the Cutting Areas

In order to achieve a 6-millimeter-long cutting stroke, two adjacent lengthwise areas must be simultaneously cut. And when the two areas each require differing amounts of wood to be removed, simple calculations must be made so the overlapped cutting will produce the correct thicknesses of the two areas.

Illustration 26 shows the marking-and-cutting procedure. In this illustration the cutting details are lightly penciled on the reed. But as experience has been gained, it will be found that the cutting depth of two or three adjacent areas may be easily memorized. At that time the writing of numbers or codes on the reed may become unnecessary.

Illustration 26

MARKING AND CUTTING THE BLADE

The reed is positioned at a gridwork intersection while the abstract is also in plain sight; when a reed area is discovered that is thicker than the abstract specification, the area is marked for cutting as shown below; or if a reed area is discovered that is thinner than the abstract specification, the abstract is coded with a − or = sign; and when enough areas have been marked on the reed to warrant cutting, the reed is transferred to the clipboard

Contact point of micrometer stem

The crosswise witness mark is lightly penciled on the reed; the pencil point must brush the micrometer stem to position the mark accurately

The number of cutting strokes needed for the area is lightly penciled on the reed; then the next-lower area is measured and marked for any additional cutting

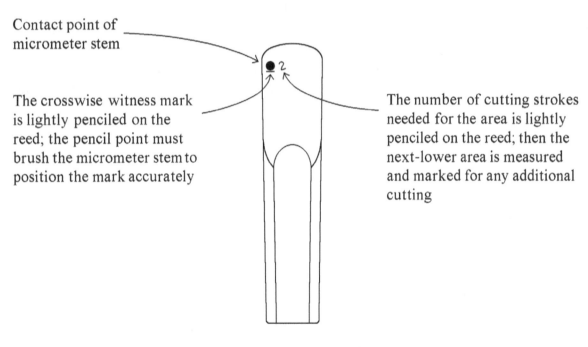

26a. Marking the blade

Continued on page 58

Although the reed is measured downwardly from the tip toward the shoulder, the cutting progresses in the opposite direction—upwardly from the lowest witness mark toward the tip

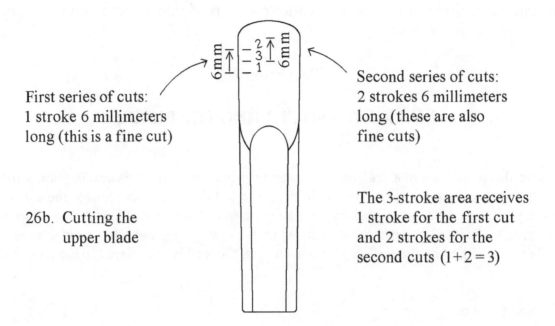

First series of cuts:
1 stroke 6 millimeters
long (this is a fine cut)

Second series of cuts:
2 strokes 6 millimeters
long (these are also
fine cuts)

26b. Cutting the
upper blade

The 3-stroke area receives
1 stroke for the first cut
and 2 strokes for the
second cuts (1+2=3)

Observe that it is the areas above or between the witness marks that must be cut to measure, not the witness marks themselves (although the marks will often be removed by the knife during cutting)

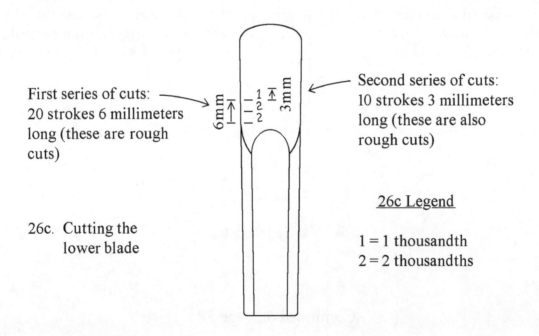

First series of cuts:
20 strokes 6 millimeters
long (these are rough
cuts)

Second series of cuts:
10 strokes 3 millimeters
long (these are also
rough cuts)

26c. Cutting the
lower blade

26c Legend

1 = 1 thousandth
2 = 2 thousandths

The lower blade is usually marked in a coded number of cutting strokes (see legend above: 10 strokes = 1 thousandth of an inch)

Updating the Abstract

If an abstract is prepared before the first break-in session, its initial coding will be marked during that session. And as the reed is modified thereafter, the abstract will also be modified to parallel the development of the reed (or the reed may be modified to parallel the development of the abstract).

Written Comments

Comments will frequently be written on the abstract as reminders about warping tendencies, reed strength, what to do on the next session, and so forth. These comments may be changed or erased in whatever manner that seems suitable.

Lower-Blade Measurements

If a reed is clipped or the backside is given extra cutting, then the measurements nearest the reed shoulder may change. And this may or may not require calculating new curves for the lower blade.

For example, if a reed is clipped to increase its strength and the thicker shoulder seems satisfactory, then new curves for the lower blade will be calculated on the abstract (the reed will be cut to the new measurements—the result will be thicker, stronger curves than before the clipping).

For another example, if a reed is given extra backside cutting to resolve a problem warp and the reed strength becomes slightly weak because of the now-thinner shoulder, then calculating new curves for the lower blade is inadvisable. Instead, the lower-blade section of the abstract will be coded with − and = signs (however, a comment might be written on the abstract that the reed should be clipped during the next session).

Additionally, if the lower blade is playing too stiffly, new lower-blade curves progressing toward a thinner shoulder may be calculated on the abstract. And when the lower blade is cut to the new measurements, it can be seen that the development of the reed can be made to parallel the development of the abstract.

Imaginary Measurements

If the reed is clipped or an area of the blade becomes expanded, then a – sign may be erased; or a = sign may become a – sign (because the area is now thicker).

Intentional Variations

As the reed gains playing hours, its characteristics will evolve. So circled variation numbers may be changed or returned to the ideal measurement numbers in any manner that seems appropriate.

Cutting-Stroke Codes

The cutting resistance may also change as the reed is played (the resistance may become greater or lesser—usually lesser as the reed gains extreme playing age). And the cutting-stroke codes may receive periodic updating as the need is discovered.

❖   ❖   ❖

VII. THE UPPER BLADE

The principal function of the upper blade is to establish the tone quality (the secondary function is to contribute to the reed stiffness), and this can be controlled by the player.

The technique is begun by selecting reeds of the correct density (or strength rating) for your mouthpiece and embouchure. Then the upper blades of these reeds will all receive the same, identical shape of cut that has proved most successful for

Illustration 27

AREA DIVISIONS OF THE UPPER BLADE

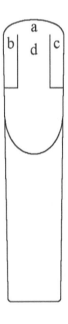

The upper left edge (b), the upper right edge (c), and the upper reed heart (d) combine their bending resistances to establish the stiffness of the upper blade; the reed tip (a) also contributes stiffness but is considered a separate area because its crosswise actions may be more important than its lengthwise actions

your playing style. The reason why this system works is when the density and cut are closely matched from reed to reed, the spring-bending rates, water-loaded inertia rates, and resonance qualities will also be closely matched from reed to reed.

When applying this system, it will be found that the manufacturer's strength rating is only an approximation of what is needed for your playing style. And since it is impossible for the manufacturer to cut reeds to your specific requirements (or to keep them in that shape once the warping and swelling have appeared), this responsibility must be accepted by the player.

The upper blade can be successfully adjusted by either the empirical method or the micrometer method. The empirical method will use a model reed (a new reed that has superior performance qualities in its upper blade) to evaluate the upper-edge thickness curves of the project reed (the reed that is being adjusted). When the profile views of the upper edges are directly compared between the two reeds, thick areas may be discovered in the project reed. The project reed will then be cut to resemble the model reed as closely as possible.

The thickness of the reed tip will also be adjusted at this time. But since a model reed cannot be used to evaluate the reed tip, this area will be adjusted by guesswork according to the principles detailed in this section.

When the upper edges and reed tip have been adjusted by the empirical method, they will form a framework around the upper reed heart as shown in Illustration 28a. At that time the embouchure may be used to find any extra wood in the upper-heart area.

The micrometer method offers a substantial improvement over the empirical method because the upper edges and reed tip can be designed to micrometer specifications and adjusted to tolerances of less than 1/2 thousandth of an inch in thickness. And with a little additional work, the quarter lines and centerline of the upper blade may also be cut to exact specifications shown in Illustration 28b.

The Reed Tip

The Outline of the Tip Edge

If the tip edge has a slightly crooked cut or if the upper corners are too pointed for your preference, the edge may be easily reshaped with a 2 1/2-inch-by-4-inch piece of No. 400 wet-or-dry sandpaper. To adjust the shape, hold the reed in one hand and the sandpaper in the other. Then allow the loose end of the sandpaper to flap squarely against the tip-edge rail in a brush-like manner. Be sure to adjust both the front and back views of the tip.

Illustration 28

FRAMING THE UPPER HEART

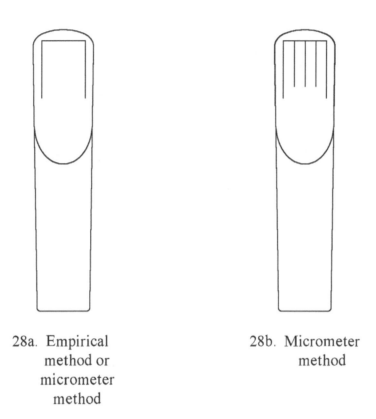

28a. Empirical
method or
micrometer
method

28b. Micrometer
method

The Thickness of the Tip

The thickness of the tip is a critical factor throughout every aspect of the performance—including tonal and dynamic ranges, precise attacks and releases, and rapid movement between registers. The reed-tip thickness (and heart-tip thickness) is also interdependently related to the mass of wood in the lower blade as described in the illusion of the reed tip on page 65. But before studying this illusion, it is necessary to understand the effects of a tip that is too thick or too thin.

The ideal measurement. There is an ideal tip-thickness measurement for each individual mouthpiece/embouchure combination, and this measurement should be applied to all reeds that are comprised of medium-density cane. When the tip is cut to this measurement, the reed will play with its greatest freedom and dependability. The micrometer measurement points are located on the crosswise 3-millimeter line at the 3/3, 3/0, and 3/3 intersections as displayed by the small dots in Illustration 29.[18]

Illustration 29

MEASUREMENT POINTS FOR THE REED TIP

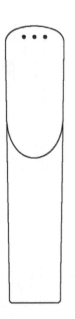

Micrometer method:

The reed tip is measured at the 3/3, 3/0, and 3/3 intersections as shown by the small dots

Tip too thick. When the tip is too thick, the tone will also be too thick; and the pitch of the low register from C1 to C2 may be sharp. Since the low register is the fundamental upon which all scales and intervals are based, this is clearly an unacceptable situation. To correct this problem, the tip will be thinned to the ideal measurement. Then the tone will be more centered, and the scales and intervals will be in much better alignment.

Tip too thin. When the tip is too thin, the tone will also be too thin; and a stress-riser condition may be present.

---

[18] *The tip edge is not used for the measurement points because it contributes no strength to the lengthwise curves of the blade.*

A stress riser is a term describing the lengthwise section wherein a thicker area (a hill) lies next to a thinner area (a valley).[19] When this happens, the thick area may transfer its stress loads into the thinner area. And instead of the reed bending evenly around the mouthpiece facing, the reed will fold at its thinner area.

A too-thin reed tip merging into the heart tip can be a serious stress-riser situation. This incorrect merging can cause a variety of problems; such as, the production of squeaks and squawks, the high notes cutting out, and the pitch going flat at loud dynamic levels. To correct this problem, the reed will be clipped until the ideal thickness measurement for the reed tip has been reached. Then the upper edges will be recut and the heart tip worked down to its best-playing shape (ideal measurements may also be developed for the heart tip).

The illusion of the reed tip. The illusion is caused by the interdependent proportions of wood between the lower blade and the reed tip. Correct interpretation of this relationship can prevent needless adjustments at the wrong end of the blade:

1. IF THE PROPORTION OF WOOD IN THE LOWER BLADE IS TOO GREAT, THEN A PROPERLY SHAPED REED TIP AND HEART TIP MAY FEEL TOO THIN; AND

2. IF THE PROPORTION OF WOOD IN THE LOWER BLADE IS TOO SMALL, THEN A PROPERLY SHAPED REED TIP AND HEART TIP MAY FEEL TOO THICK.

To understand how the first part of the illusion works, consider a player who encounters a reed in which the tip feels too thin but is actually the right thickness. This player unknowingly decides to clip the reed to correct the problem; and suddenly, a potentially good reed has become unplayable. The player might conclude that the clip

---

[19] *Stress risers are commonly found in reed blades. They can be long, lengthwise waves on the surface created by files or rush; or they can be short facets created by the reed knife. Actually, stress risers are not necessarily destructive to the performance and might even be considered a source of pleasant buzzing in the tone. But the more severely they are formed and the closer to the reed tips they are positioned, the more trouble stress risers can cause.*

was too large, but this is not so. The real solution to the problem would have been to remove some wood from the lower blade. Then the proportions of wood between the reed tip and the lower blade would be in better balance, and the tip would feel more nearly correct even though it received no adjustment at all.

The second part of the illusion most often appears through too much cutting of the primary warp. That is, as wood is slowly removed from the backside of the lower blade, a properly shaped reed tip may feel thicker and thicker. If the situation becomes too severe, the reed must be clipped to bring more wood into the lower blade. Then the upper blade must be recut to its proper specifications.

The Upper Corners

To provide smooth and even flowing as the reed tip waves from left to right and back again, the harder wood in the upper corners (at the 3/6 and 3/6 intersections) should be thinner than the softer wood in the reed-tip center.

Table 6

SAMPLE ABSTRACTS FOR THE
UPPER CORNERS AND REED TIP

	6	3	0	3	6
3	6	6+	6+	6+	6

6a. 6+ tip

	6	3	0	3	6
3	6+	7	7	7	6+

6b. 7 tip

66

When to cut the upper corners. The upper corners may be cut as part of the upper edges or as part of the reed tip. But whichever tactic you decide to use for a particular reed, be extremely careful not to remove too much wood because the upper corners are very easy to overcut. Even when being very careful, though, one or both upper corners may turn out a half-thousandth of an inch thinner than planned. But this is usually all right.

Profiling the Tip Edge

If any areas of the tip edge are too thick, then the crosswise waving of the reed tip may be impaired; and the tone quality may become thick or clouded (oppositely, slight bevels or thin areas may be acceptable). But the thick tip-edge areas can be quickly cut to an ideal measurement by using the tip-edge profiler (which is detailed on the next two pages) and a flexible piece of flattened rush.

How much wood to remove. The tip edge at the centerline and quarter-line areas should be cut until it is flush with the metal feeler gauge. However, since the front view of the tip edge curves downwardly from the 0-millimeter line, the areas just above the edge lines should remain slightly thicker than the feeler gauge.

Selecting the feeler-gauge thickness. The tip-edge thickness best matched to your mouthpiece and embouchure must be found by experiment. These experiments are easy to perform, and some of your existing reeds may serve as examples of nearly matched tip edges.

And generally, the tip edge might be between .004 inch and .007 inch.

If the tone is too thick or if the response is too slow, the tip-edge measurement should be reduced by 1/2 thousandth of an inch.

If the tone is too thin, the tip-edge measurement should be increased by 1/2 thousandth of an inch.[20]

---

[20] *Feeler gauges are available in sets, and in these sets the gauges are usually graduated in increments of whole thousandths of an inch (be sure to read the package to see which thicknesses are enclosed). But a .0015-inch feeler should also be included. So a .0045" gauge can be assembled by stacking a .003" feeler on top of the .0015" feeler. Or a .0055" gauge can be assembled by stacking a .004" feeler on top of the .0015" feeler.*

Illustration 30

THE TIP-EDGE PROFILER

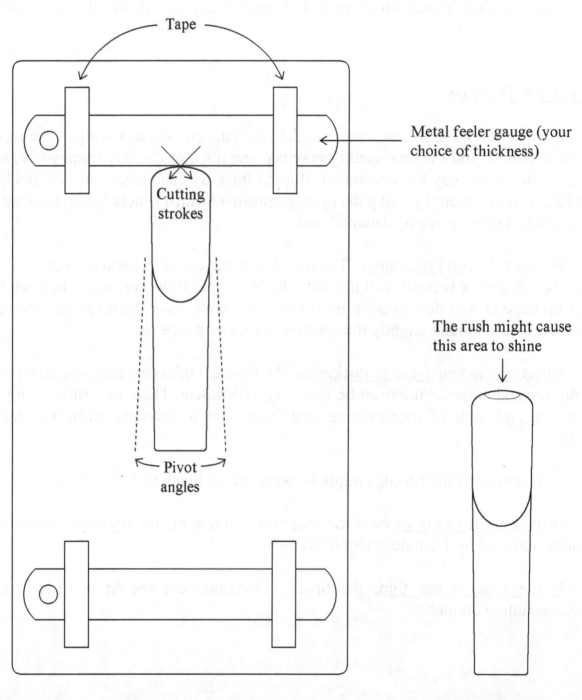

Tape

Metal feeler gauge (your choice of thickness)

Cutting strokes

The rush might cause this area to shine

Pivot angles

30a. The profiling tool

30b. The tip-edge cutting area

Table 7

CONSTRUCTION AND USE OF THE TIP-EDGE PROFILER

Construction

1. The base plate is a flat piece of metal or plastic; the backside may be padded with a full-size piece of felt;

2. The metal feeler gauge is tightly taped to the base plate, and be careful when taping the gauge—the thin metal is fragile; and

3. A second gauge of a different thickness (to be used for special situations) may be added to the opposite end of the base plate, but the second gauge is optional.

Use

1. Slide the reed upwardly until the tip edge touches the feeler gauge; then cut the edge with a flexible piece of flattened rush; use diagonal, back-grain cutting strokes in whatever manner that is convenient—but do not allow the rush to drag over the upper corners;

2. If an extra-thick tip-edge area is discovered, some rough cutting may be done with the reed knife and clipboard;

3. When the length of the cut is limited to 2.5 millimeters, the ideal tip measurements at the 3-millimeter line will not be altered (the rush might produce a glossy finish on the reed that shows the length of the cutting area);

4. In order to cut the full width of both quarter lines, the heel of the reed may be pivoted to the left and right; and

5. If it is desired to do any rushing of the reed upper corners with the tip-edge profiler, then back-grain cutting must not be used because the corner fibers might be torn apart by the rush.

<u>When to profile the tip edge</u>. The tip edge should be checked and adjusted when the reed is brand new. And obviously, the edge may need adjusting after each time the tip is clipped. But further adjustments may be needed even though the tip has not been clipped.

The tip-edge fibers are only partially supported by surrounding material, and the exposed ends of the fibers are located in the most highly active part of the reed. This means that the tip-edge fibers are very susceptible to vibration expansion and to water-absorption expansion.[21] And the tip edge should be checked and adjusted during every break-in session or practice session.

<u>Journalizing the abstract</u>. If a particular reed requires a tip edge that is different than your standard thickness, the reed abstract should be marked as shown on page 55.

<u>Profiler maintenance</u>. Eventually, the profiler will need disassembly to remove the accumulation of sawdust from beneath the feeler gauge. When removing the tape (which may have hardened with age), be extremely careful not to damage the thin, metal gauge.

<u>Conclusions</u>. The tip-edge profiler is very easy to make and use and offers a significant advantage to either the empirical method or micrometer method.

Also, players who double on various saxophones might prefer an increased range of feeler-gauge thicknesses by having more than one profiling tool.

<u>The Upper Edges</u>

<u>The Phenomenon of the Beating Reed</u>

During vibration the left reed tip rapidly accelerates toward the tip rail of the mouthpiece where it comes to a complete stop, and at the same time the right reed tip rapidly accelerates toward the maximum opening distance where it also comes to a complete stop. Then the actions reciprocate. The right reed tip accelerates toward the tip rail of the mouthpiece as the left reed tip accelerates toward the maximum opening distance.[22]

---

[21] *Additional discussion of expansion is presented on page 124.*

[22] *As negative pressure is initiated in the left side of the mouthpiece chamber, the left side of the reed will be drawn toward the mouthpiece. Concurrently, as positive pressure is initiated in the right side of the mouthpiece chamber, the right side of the reed will be pushed away from the mouthpiece.*

Illustration 31

TIP-RAIL VIEW: THE PHENOMENON
OF THE BEATING REED

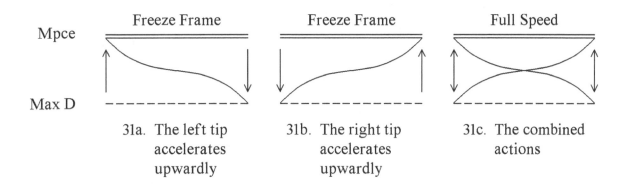

	Freeze Frame	Freeze Frame	Full Speed
Mpce			
Max D			

31a. The left tip accelerates upwardly

31b. The right tip accelerates upwardly

31c. The combined actions

The upper-edge mass. As an upper-edge mass becomes too great, the extra wood and the water it contains will require more energy from the player's breath for acceleration and bending. And as the stiffness of the reed exceeds the strength of the embouchure, the reed will be in greater control of the performance than the player.

When a stiff reed is unrestrained by the embouchure, the pivot lines will be free to bend and jerk around any thick areas or hard spots in the grain while the differing water-loaded inertia rates of the thick areas further complicate the problem. The results of these uncontrolled imbalances will be:

1. The irregular pivot lines and inertia rates will produce too much buzzing in the tone (micro-metronomic distortions);

2. The extra stiffness of the reed will contribute to slow response and to player fatigue; and

3. The pitch will be sharp.

The above problems represent the tone/strength/intonation force group discussed in the preface. And the upper-edge contribution to these problems is especially important because of the large amount of motion the edges incur during the beating of the reed. But by cutting the upper edges down to their ideal shapes, the upper-edge contribution to all three of the above problems will be corrected at the same time; and the synchronization of the paired opening/closing edges will also be improved.

Illustration 32

PROFILE VIEW: COMPARING THE UPPER-BLADE
EDGES OF THE MODEL AND PROJECT REEDS

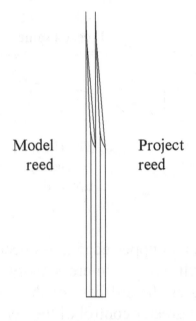

Model   Project
reed   reed

Comparing left edges

Table 8

INSTRUCTIONS FOR CUTTING THE
UPPER-BLADE EDGES BY THE EMPIRICAL METHOD

1. Unlike the cutting areas used with the micrometer method, the empirical-method cutting areas will extend upwardly only to the top witness mark (not 3 millimeters beyond the mark);

2. Do not angle the knife toward the edge of the reed to any great degree; a wide cut as shown in Illustration 33b will blend the edge into the heart;

3. The profile view of a finished upper edge should show a very slight curve from the tip to the bite line; there may be thin areas from the factory cut, but all thick areas will be trimmed down to your ideal shape; and

4. If necessary, blend the upper edges into the lower edges; but work slowly and test play the reed; too much cutting near the bite-line area can cause the pitch of some reeds to go flat.

Illustration 33

CUTTING THE UPPER-BLADE EDGES
BY THE EMPIRICAL METHOD

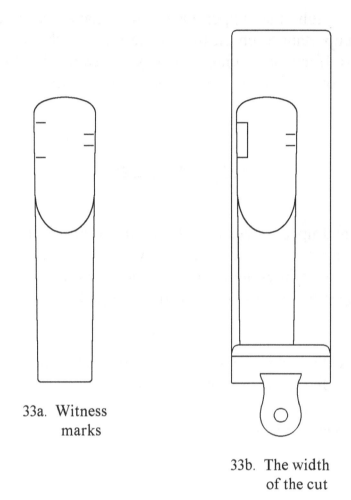

33a. Witness
marks

33b. The width
of the cut

Cutting the Upper Edges by the Empirical Method

Place the project reed on top of the model reed with the tips of both reeds perfectly aligned. Then turn the assembly to compare the left upper edges with a large magnifying glass.

Pencil a few witness marks near the left edge of the project reed to mark the borders of the thick areas and repeat the process for the right upper edge. Then the reed will be cut on the clipboard.[23]

---

[23] *If a model reed cannot be found in which both upper edges are correctly shaped, then two model reeds may be used. One model will be for the left edge, and the other will be for the right edge. The model reed (reeds) must be brand-new so that no vibration expansion will have occurred.*

Cutting the Upper Edges by the Micrometer Method

Follow the instructions given on pages 56 through 58. But remember not to angle the knife toward the edge of the reed to any great degree.

Also, even though the upper-edge lines have been cut to micrometer specifications, it is important to check the profile view of the upper-edge rails for any remaining thick areas. If any are found, they may be removed with a piece of rush (this might add resonance or brightness to the tone quality with little sacrifice in the reed strength).

The Upper Heart

When the tip and upper edges have been cut to their ideal shapes, attention may be given to the shaping of the upper heart. However, since the upper edges and upper heart combine their effects in establishing the tone and strength of the upper blade, the upper edges and upper heart must be considered together in the design of the upper blade.

The outlines in Illustration 34 show two limits that may be used in designing an upper heart, but it is likely that an intermediate shape will give the most versatile performance. In any case, the playing and flexing tests will be the final judgments in determining the best shape for the upper heart, not the visual test of observing the heart outline.

Rainbow Shape

This shape is characterized by a thick, wide heart tip that tapers steeply toward thin upper side rails (and possibly a thin tip edge). The thin rails will produce a well-centered tone while the stiff heart provides the strength, and the heart resistance to twisting will provide the buzzing in the sound.

The disadvantages of the rainbow shape are that the tone quality may be too refined for all-around performance. Or if the side rails become too thin, an incurable rattle may develop in the sound. Also, this design is most vulnerable to a destructive upper-blade primary warp (on page 77).

74

Christmas Tree Shape

This shape is characterized by a narrow heart tip that mildly tapers toward thicker edges and side rails than the rainbow shape. The thicker edges bear more responsibility for maintaining the upper-blade strength and for buzzing the sound.

The disadvantage of the Christmas tree shape is that the tone quality may be too rough for all-around performance.

Intermediate Shape

An intermediate shape will be the probable choice for most players because of the wide range of tone colors available by manipulating the blowing style.

Illustration 34

TWO LIMITS IN DESIGNING AN UPPER HEART

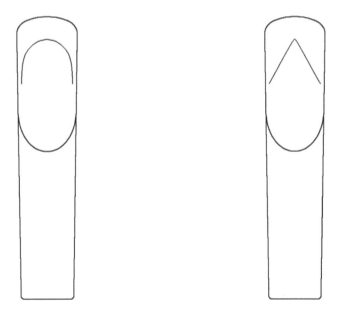

34a. Rainbow shape   34b. Christmas tree shape

Empirical Tests for the Upper Blade

Flexing tests. The stiffness of the upper edges and reed tip can be tested by placing the reed between the pads of the thumb and forefinger and flexing the reed back and forth.

The stiffness of the heart outline may also be tested with the reed between the thumb and forefinger, but for this test squeeze the reed hard enough to bring the finger bones into play while flexing the reed.

Along the heart outline there should be a definite increase in stiffness, and the stiffness should increase even more as the heart outline approaches the bite line.

Playing tests. When using the micrometer method, the upper heart may be cut to your preferred measurements (or sometimes a little thinner) without too much danger of overcutting the reed. But when using the empirical method, the upper heart may be left a little stiff as insurance against removing too much wood (the reed may then break in naturally as playing time is gained). If an upper heart is playing much too stiffly, however, it should not receive a random scraping. Instead, the embouchure may be used to test the areas in Illustration 35.

Illustration 35

EMPIRICAL AREA DIVISIONS FOR THE UPPER HEART

<u>Heart tip too thick</u>. When the heart tip is too thick, the reed will be difficult to set into vibration. Begin by thinning the upper parts of Areas 1 and 2.

<u>Heart tip too wide</u>. When the heart tip is too wide, middle D (fourth line in the treble clef) may have a rough or clouded tone.[24] To repair this condition, the outer edges of Areas 1 and 2 may be lightly thinned to produce more of a Christmas tree shape.

<u>Lower areas too thick</u>. Area 5 is located at the center of the bite line and may be thinned to reduce the strength and blowing resistance of the entire reed. After this area is thinned, the embouchure might make a better evaluation of other adjustments needed in a stiff-playing upper blade.

The cutting of Area 5, though, might change the lengthwise position of the bite line. But the bite line can be easily repositioned by additional cutting. To shorten the bite, elongate the cut area toward the upper-blade side of the reed. Or to lengthen the bite, elongate the cut area toward the lower-blade side of the reed.

<u>Lower areas too wide</u>. The increased stiffness of the heart outline as it approaches the left and right sides of the bite line is necessary to provide a "lock" for consistent intonation. But too much wood in these areas can cause a rigid tone and a possible sharpening in pitch. If it seems appropriate to do so, a light cutting of the outer parts of Areas 3 and 4 might make the reed much easier to play.

The Upper-Blade Primary Warp

The primary warp will extend into the upper blade. But the upper-blade section of the warp, from the bite line to the heart tip, should be considered a separate area because it presents different performance problems than the lower-area primary warp.

One point to remember is that the upper-blade primary warp is a common and natural occurrence. And if a moderate warp is causing no performance problems, then intentional repair is unnecessary and inadvisable.

---

[24] *The playing test for a wide heart tip may be correctly evaluated while the reed is in its dynamic shape. But if any confusion is experienced, a better evaluation might be made if the reed is test played in its static shape.*

It will also be seen that as the reed is dynamically balanced, the backside sanding will automatically extend farther and farther into the upper blade (see Illustration 10 on page 18) even though the finger pressure remains located at the reed shoulder. And the slight upper-blade thinning incurred during dynamic balancing may be all the adjustment that a particular reed might require.

Symptoms

When this warp develops, the entire upper heart may function as a stress riser working in opposition to the efforts of the upper edges and reed tip. That is, when the reed is placed into vibration, the warp-reinforced upper heart may attempt to remain motionless.

The problems involved with this warp can be very severe; such as, the reed may refuse to vibrate (which might cause an unpleasant tone), the reed strength may feel much too stiff (when it actually may not be), or the high F and low Bb may be extremely out of tune.

Checking for an Upper-Blade Primary Warp

With the reed flat side up, aim the tip of the reed directly into the lamp, a few inches away from the bulb. Then rock and slide the 6-inch ruler from the lower blade toward the reed tip. It will also be necessary to observe the lengthwise position of greatest warping (crosswise curvature) so that the finger pressure may be applied at that point when sanding the warp.

This check may be made while the reed is in its static shape or in its dynamic shape. But if the reed is in its static shape, the upper blade must be moistened and the wrinkles pressed out of the tip before the check is made.

Solutions

When the warp is found in the static shape, test play the reed for a few, quick notes to see if a problem is actually being presented (if not, leave the warp alone for now).

Static shape: The warp is presenting problems. 1 to 3 cutting strokes (your choice, your risk) may be applied in the static shape; when the warp is cut in the static shape, the full impact in the reed strength will be immediately realized.

Dynamic shape: The warp is presenting problems. 3 to 10 cutting strokes (your choice, your risk) may be applied in the dynamic shape; when the warp is cut in the dynamic shape, the full impact in the reed strength may not be realized until the next playing session.

To cut the warp, use the No. 400 sandpaper on the surface plate. Now with the finger pressure at the correct lengthwise position, apply the cutting strokes. And be careful to keep the finger pressure at the vertical centerline of the reed. Upper-blade sanding must never be offset to the left or right sides. Then the backside may be lightly polished on the flat file while the finger pressure is centered on the reed shoulder.

Illustration 36

SANDING THE BACKSIDE OF AN
UPPER-BLADE PRIMARY WARP

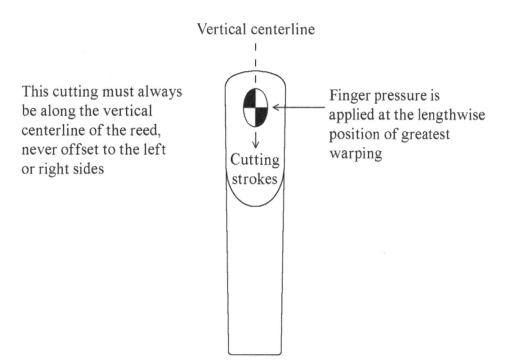

Vertical centerline

This cutting must always be along the vertical centerline of the reed, never offset to the left or right sides

Cutting strokes

Finger pressure is applied at the lengthwise position of greatest warping

Static shape: 1 to 3 cutting strokes (your choice, your risk) may be applied; when the warp is cut in the static shape, the full impact in the reed strength will be immediately realized

Dynamic shape: 3 to 10 cutting strokes (your choice, your risk) may be applied; when the warp is cut in the dynamic shape, the full impact in the reed strength may not be realized until the next playing session

Redesigning the Upper Blade

The source of the upper-blade primary warp is the same as that detailed on page 11 for the lower-area warp; that is, the cross section center of mass is too far away from the cross section centerline (although the internal tension of the cane fibers may also contribute to warping the thin wood—sometimes moderate, sometimes severe). Redesigning the front side of the upper blade into a slightly flatter crosswise curve will bring the center of mass and centerline closer together, which should reduce the potential of the upper-blade primary warp.

The upper edges may be left a bit thicker than your ideal measurements (or the edges may be allowed to expand—clipping the tip will also thicken the upper edges).

Increasing the upper-edge thickness is best suited for reeds in which the density is too low (soft cane).

The upper heart may receive additional thinning provided that the cane is not too soft. The empirical method may be applied by guesswork, and test playings will be needed as the cutting progresses. But the micrometer method allows the entire upper heart to be modified before the test playing.

Within the new design the heart tip at the 6/6, 6/0, and 6/6 intersections may be reduced by 1/2 thousandth of an inch from your ideal measurements. And the micrometer-method bite line at the 15/3, 15/0, and 15/3 intersections may be reduced by 1 thousandth of an inch from your ideal measurements.[25] Then new curves will be plotted from the redesigned heart tip to the redesigned bite line.

An example of this method is shown on page 82.

Delayed Action

When a reed has been played into its dynamic shape and then allowed to rest for a few minutes (either on or off the mouthpiece), the upper blade may develop a pronounced primary warp. If the warp seems to be causing too much trouble, toss the reed out.

---

[25] *Reducing the ideal measurements by the above-stated amounts is only a suggestion, not a rule.*

How the Upper-Blade Warp Affects the Tip Cutting

When a warped reed tip is knifed on the clipboard, it will not be possible to knife the tip center (at the 3/0 intersection) completely to measure without removing too much wood from the adjacent areas. So the tip center must be finished with an alternate cutting tool.

As a reminder about this condition, the abstract measurement number for this intersection may be enclosed in a three-sided bracket.

Conclusions

The upper-blade primary warp may be repaired by removing wood from the backside of the upper heart or from the front side of the upper heart.

Sanding the backside is an easy repair. But if too much wood is removed, the reed might then develop an irreparable upper-blade concave warp. Or the grain structure of the sanded area may become sheared off at too steep an angle, which can cause uncooperative vibrating actions around the heart tip.

Cutting the upper-heart front side is a more complicated procedure. But since the backside shear angle will not be increased, this method might produce a better-playing reed.

The micrometer method is both quicker and safer than the empirical method when making the front-side repair. When using either method, the backside may still require some sanding as a final adjustment.

After the primary warp has been repaired, the upper-blade strength may become weaker than you prefer. But this may nevertheless be the best configuration for the reed. As a compensation for a weakened upper blade, the tip may be clipped to bring more wood into the lower blade.

Table 9

DESIGNING THINNER UPPER-HEART MEASUREMENTS TO CORRECT AN UPPER-BLADE PRIMARY WARP

	6	3	0	3	6
3	6	6+	6+	6+	6
6	9+	11	11+	11	9+
9	13+	16+	17	16+	13+
12	18	22+	23	22+	18
15	23	29	31	29	23
18	29				29

9a. Ideal measurements

	6	3	0	3	6
3	6	6+	6+	6+	6
6	9+	(10+)	(11)	(10+)	9+
9	13+		PW		13+
12	18				18
15	23	(28)	(30)	(28)	23
18	29				29

9b. Thinned upper-heart measurement points

	6	3	0	3	6
3	6	6+	[6+]	6+	6
6	9+	(10+) 5+	11 6 [P̶W̶]	(10+) 5+	9+
9	13+	16 6	17 6+	16 6	13+
12	18	22 6	23+ 6+	22 6	18
15	23	(28)	(30)	(28)	23
18	29				29

9c. New lengthwise curves have been plotted on the abstract

Table 10

CODING THE ABSTRACT FOR AN UPPER-BLADE PRIMARY WARP

The following codes may be marked in the upper-blade section of the abstract

| PW | The primary warp is causing problems |

| P̶W̶ | The problems have been resolved, but the crossed-out code may remain on the abstract as a reminder about the tendency of the reed |

| DAPW | A delayed-reaction primary warp is present but is not causing severe problems at this time (if the problems were severe, the reed and its abstract would probably be tossed out) |

| 6+ | The 3/0 intersection is enclosed in a three-sided bracket as a reminder that the area should not be completely knifed on the clipboard to avoid overcutting the adjacent areas |

| (10+) | Intentional variations from the ideal measurements are enclosed in a circle |

The Upper-Blade Angle

When the upper blade sets into a curve along the mouthpiece facing or after the backside has been recut, the reed tip (at its open-most position) may be too close to the mouthpiece tip. The closed-up tip might constrict the player's breath, the reed strength may feel too weak (when it actually may not be), or the high F may become flat while the low Bb becomes sharp.

Fortunately, the adjustment for this problem is easy and risk-free: simply bend the reed away from the mouthpiece-facing curve.

Resetting the Upper-Blade Angle

The bending must be along the vertical centerline while the wetted reed is pinched between the thumb and forefinger: (1) the first bending area is placed just above the bite line and receives the greatest amount of bending; (2) the second area is placed just above the first and receives a lesser amount of bending than the first area; and (3) the third area is placed just above the second and receives the same amount of bending as the second area.

When the reed is returned to vibration, the upper blade will once again begin to curve along the mouthpiece facing. But this time the upper-blade angle may set at a more open position than before the bending adjustment.

How Far To Reset the Upper-Blade Angle

Minimum bend. For a newer reed or for a reed of the correct strength, the tip may be opened 1/16 or 1/8 inch from its closed-up position. But it is impractical and unnecessary actually to measure the distance.

Medium bend. If the reed strength proves to be too weak, then a more open bend might be applied. Or the tip might be clipped to strengthen the blade.

Maximum bend. Bends of 1/4 inch or more should be reserved only for reeds that have reached their very last phase of usefulness because the fibers will stretch and crack when bent to the maximum.

Illustration 37

RESETTING THE UPPER-BLADE ANGLE

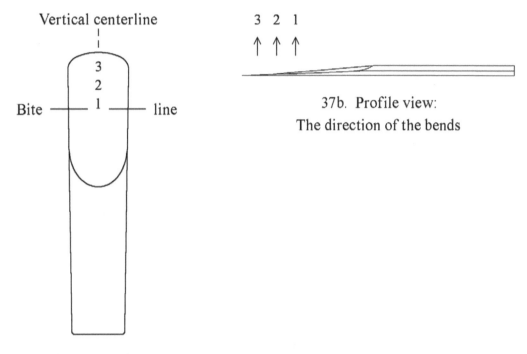

37a. Front view:

The relation to the bite line
and vertical centerline

37b. Profile view:
The direction of the bends

Instructions

1. The first area (just above the bite line) receives the greatest
   amount of bending

2. The second area receives less bending than the first area; and

3. The third area receives the same amount of bending as the
   second area

Note: The bending adjustment must always be performed on a wetted reed, never
on a dry reed

❖   ❖   ❖

VIII. THE LOWER BLADE

The lower blade, which extends from the bite line to the shoulder edge, is the most interesting and complex area of reed adjustment. When one aspect of interdependence is adjusted, the others will also be changed to some degree.

Although the principal function of the lower blade is to establish the strength and pitch of the reed, the lower blade also contributes to the tone quality.[26] But the tone quality is secondary in the design of the lower blade just as strength and pitch are secondary in the design of the upper blade.

The lower blade may be adjusted by the empirical method or by the micrometer method. The empirical method will be applied by estimating how much wood to remove from suspected thick areas according to the principles detailed in this section. Although the empirical method will not produce the even lengthwise curves of the micrometer method, empirical cutting can produce excellent results. The micrometer method will use simple, mathematic lengthwise curves for the lower blade. Although these curves will be more even than those produced by the empirical method, the lower blade will still not be perfectly shaped because of the thinning effect of backside sanding.

When working with the lower blade, the first adjustments will be to remove the gross imbalances, such as, flattening the backside or cutting down an extra-thick edge; and the reed should play much better. The performance qualities may then be analyzed for other areas of improvement. But since any further lower-blade cutting will have several simultaneous effects, the player must be thoroughly familiar with each of the aspects of interdependence, some of which may be very important to the performance of a particular reed and some of which may not.

---

[26] *The ways in which the lower areas contribute to the tone quality include establishing a centered pivot point and straight pivot lines and by regulating the amount of ringing in the sound. A well-designed lower blade also assists in achieving a comfortable embouchure that is necessary for tonal shading and flexibility.*

Interdependence and the Lower Blade

In order to simplify this section, it will be assumed that the upper blade has been cut to the ideal micrometer measurements for your mouthpiece and embouchure and that the reed has no substantial problems within its cane. After this material has been studied, the summary on page 92 may be used for quick reference.

1. Tone, strength, and intonation: Within this force group the lower blade is largely responsible for the strength and pitch of the reed. Although the pitch is most important, exact intonation cannot be properly evaluated unless the strength is within the range that is acceptable to the embouchure;

   Generally, a large amount of wood will be removed from the lower blade when reflattening the backside; as a result, the strength will become weaker and the pitch will become flatter;[27]

   If the player is willing to accept a partial air leak, the backside cutting may be terminated before the reed reaches a critical weakening point; however, many players may discover that a leak-free backside is mandatory for their blowing styles; and additional backside cutting will be needed;

   When this extra cutting is performed, the strength and pitch may decline to unacceptable levels; and the reed must then be clipped and the upper blade recut to its proper specifications;

   The clipping-and-upper-blade-recutting procedure can become a time-consuming inconvenience if it must be performed too many times during a single break-in session; beginning with a half-strength-harder reed might avoid some of this recutting;

---

[27] *The weakening/flattening effect described above may be related to any wood removed from the blade. But remember that a hard-blowing reed and sharpness in the pitch are two major symptoms of the primary and tangent warps. Therefore, the removal of backside wood may have a greater effect on the strength and pitch than removing wood from the lower-blade front side. This is strong evidence as to why dynamic balancing of the cross section should be one of the first adjustments made to the reed during each break-in session.*

The initial strength and pitch of a harder reed will be stiff and sharp; and as the primary and/or tangent warps begin to develop, the reed will play even stiffer and sharper; but as wood is removed from the reed back during dynamic balancing, the strength should fall into the normal range for your embouchure, at which time the pitch may be properly evaluated;

After the backside has been recut in each break-in session, any additional cutting of the lower-blade front side will further reduce the strength and further lower the pitch;

2. The bite-line position: If the proportion of wood in the lower blade is too great, then a short bite will result; or if the proportion of wood in the lower blade is too small (or if the shoulder edge is too far away from the reed tip), then a long bite will result;

Backside warping can also have a profound effect on the bite-line position (the primary and tangent warps will lengthen the bite, and an occasional dynamic-shape concave warp may have an unpredictable or inconsistent bite); therefore, the length of the bite cannot be properly evaluated until the backside has been reflattened during that break-in session;

After the reflattening, the lower blade may require additional cutting to balance other forces in the reed; and this cutting will serve to lengthen the bite; this lengthening will be acceptable as long as no embouchure discomfort is created;

3. The concave and primary warps: Removing wood from the lower-blade center area (Area f in Illustration 38 on the following page) will increase the tendency for the concave warp; and removing wood from the lower-blade outer areas (Areas e and g) will increase the tendency for the primary warp; these effects are generally true whether the wood is removed from the front side or backside;

If the lower-blade outer areas are too thick, cutting them down to approximate normal thickness will move the center of mass away from the cross section centerline; and the tendency for the primary warp will be increased; this is all right if the outer-area cutting is performed during the early break-in sessions because the primary warping will be eliminated through the routine cutting of the backside;

Illustration 38

AREA DIVISIONS OF THE LOWER BLADE

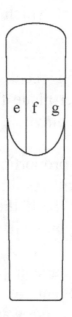

But if the outer-area cutting is delayed until after the backside warping has stabilized, the warping/reflattening process may start up again; and if the additional reflattening happens to be too severe, this in turn might lead to a large clipping of the tip and a complete rebalancing of the entire blade;

Another condition exists when only one edge is too thick and is not quickly cut down to approximate normal thickness; when this happens, the warping actions may gravitate toward the thicker side of the reed (the stock can also play a role in this condition); and the backside edge gap may be larger on the thicker side of the reed; this is not necessarily a destructive feature because the offset-cutting technique (on page 16) may be used; but it is possible that more break-in sessions than necessary will be performed to stabilize the warping, which is contrary to the goal of a quick-cut reed;

Additional adjusting of well-balanced lower blades may need only small amounts of cutting; and being small amounts, little effect may be found in the warping actions;

4. <u>The illusion of the reed tip</u>: If the proportion of wood in the lower blade is too great, then a properly shaped reed tip and heart tip may feel too thin; or if the proportion of wood in the lower blade is too small, then a properly shaped reed tip and heart tip may feel too thick;

   This means that as wood is gradually removed from the lower blade (from either the front or back sides), the tip may feel thicker and thicker; or the entire upper blade may begin to feel too thick.

High-Note/Low-Note Balancing

This is the fifth and final aspect of interdependence, and the goal of this balancing is to enable the highest and lowest notes to be played without excess manipulation of the embouchure and without increasing the blowing pressure:

5a. IF THE PROPORTION OF WOOD IN THE LOWER BLADE IS TOO GREAT (OR IF THE SHOULDER EDGE IS TOO CLOSE TO THE REED TIP), THEN THE LOW Bb MAY BE DIFFICULT TO PRODUCE; AND

5b. IF THE PROPORTION OF WOOD IN THE LOWER BLADE IS TOO SMALL (OR IF THE SHOULDER EDGE IS TOO FAR AWAY FROM THE REED TIP), THEN THE HIGH F MAY CRACK OR CUT OUT.

This can be a very difficult adjustment because many otherwise-excellent reeds will not respond to the complete tonal range of the instrument.[28]

---

[28] *Since cutting out of the highest and lowest notes is also a major symptom of a warped reed, the backside should be checked for air leaks before adjusting the blade. Also, a few more polishing strokes on the flat file might help the reed performance even though the back already appears to be quite flat.*

Table 11

SUMMARY OF LOWER-BLADE CUTTING

Each time the lower blade is cut, the following aspects will be simultaneously changed, some with great effect and some with little effect according to the nature of that individual reed; also, to simplify this summary, it is assumed that the upper blade has been cut to the ideal measurements for your mouthpiece and embouchure and that no substantial problems are present within the cane

Section A: Interdependent Aspects

Tone, Strength, and Intonation	The Bite-Line Position	The Concave and Primary Warps	The Illusion of the Reed Tip	High-Note/ Low-Note Balancing
The strength will become weaker, and the pitch will become lower; the finished reed strength must be acceptable to the embouchure; pitch is most important	The bite may become slightly longer; this is often an insignificant aspect in a dynamically balanced reed	These warps will be slightly amplified according to where and how much wood is removed; all adjustments should be performed as soon as possible	The reed tip (or the entire upper blade) might feel slightly thicker; this can be a significant or insignificant aspect	The low notes might play easier, and the high notes might cut out; this can be a significant or insignificant aspect

Section B: Secondary Aspects

The Pivot Lines	Resonance and Projection
The embouchure may gain greater control over bent or crooked pivot lines	These qualities may be increased up to a certain point; then they may begin to decrease

How the High-F Problem Develops

As wood is removed from the lower blade or shoulder edge, which is often done to improve the response of the low notes, the high F may begin to cut out.

How To Correct the Problem

A small clipping of the reed tip and a minor recutting of the upper blade will usually restore the high F.

Evaluations of the Lower Blade

Since each piece of cane will display its own individual nature, the lower blades of your reeds may evolve to slightly different shapes as their performance problems are resolved.

The lengthwise position of the shoulder edge and its thickness at that position is a major factor in establishing the strength and pitch of the reed. The lengthwise curves from the bite line to the shoulder edge are also important because the shape and mass of wood in these areas contribute to all aspects of the reed performance.

When using the micrometer method, any extra wood in the lower blade will be discovered by direct measurement; and as a supplement, the profile views of the lower-blade side rails will be regularly checked.

When using the empirical method, the profile views of the lower-blade side rails will be the principal method of evaluation; and this may be supplemented by observing the outline of the lower heart.

Illustration 39

PROFILE VIEWS: THE LOWER-BLADE SIDE RAILS

39a. Nearly straight

Although this shape is most resistant to the primary warp, the extra wood in the lower-blade side rails and edge lines will make this reed play stiff and sharp while the damping effect of the extra wood may produce a dull sound; the low register will be difficult to play; and the tone quality will be inflexible as compared to the curved section in 39b

39b. Curved

The curved section is probably the best choice; this shape will provide a resonant tone in all registers while maintaining proper support and fast response; the primary and concave warps should assume their normal dimensions

39c. Notched

Notching the lower part of the side rails may increase the resonance and weaken the strength, which may be helpful when working on a stiff piece of cane; the primary and concave warps may assume greater dimensions than a curved section

39d. Nearly parallel

When the lower-blade edge rails are thinned nearly to the shoulder, the lower heart may need to be thickened to maintain support; this shape can produce an extremely bright and resonant tone; thin lower side rails can create a rattling in the sound, but unlike the permanent rattling associated with thin upper side rails, this rattle might disappear in time; finally, the nearly parallel section with a thick lower heart is guaranteed to cause the greatest problems with the primary warp

Filing the Shoulder Edge

During the adjustment of a particular reed, you may begin to suspect that the shoulder edge is too close to the reed tip (or too high on the profile if you prefer to think of it in that way). This speculation might be because the low notes are playing too stiffly or because the reed is lacking in resonance even though in both cases the blade seems to be correctly shaped. Also, the bite may feel too short.

In determining the correct lengthwise position for the shoulder edge, there is a specific playing test that can be made. The playing test is to check the intonation of the low Bb.[29]

Checking for a Sharp Low Bb

If all other routine adjustments have been made and the low Bb is playing sharp, the shoulder edge may be filed to improve the resonance, response, and intonation of the reed.

How To File the Shoulder Edge

The equaling file. This broad-tipped needle file has a long, rectangular shape and is flat on both sides; and the file selected should have medium- or wide-spaced teeth. These files are usually available only with single-cut teeth, not criss-crossed teeth. But single-cut teeth are all right for this procedure.

The advantage in using the equaling file is in its flexibility (and it does not have a pointed tip that would gouge the wood). This file can be bent against the reed during cutting to maintain a nearly sharp shoulder edge. And a nearly sharp shoulder edge is necessary to provide a "lock" for consistent intonation.

To file the edge, press the reed firmly against a flat scrap of plastic (or whatever) while bending the file against the shoulder. Apply 10 or 12 short cutting strokes beginning at the left edge and ending at the right edge. Then apply another 10 or 12 short cutting strokes beginning at the right edge and ending at the left edge (illustrated on the following page).

---

[29] Also, see Table 15 on page 123.

Illustration 40

FILING THE SHOULDER EDGE

File upwardly along the slash marks from left to right, then from right to left; keep the equaling file bent against the reed to maintain a nearly sharp shoulder edge

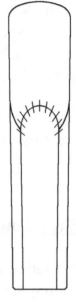

40a. Standard stock   40b. Thinned stock

Checking the Cutting Area

Hold the reed up to the lamp to observe the shiny area created by the file. You may decide to apply a few more cutting strokes for sake of appearance.

The Effects of Filing the Shoulder Edge

The resonance. The ringing in the sound will probably be increased throughout the entire tonal range of the instrument, not just in the low notes.

The strength. The reed strength may be slightly weakened, or there may be no noticeable change.

The bite line. The bite may become slightly longer, or there may be no change at all.

Limited effect. If the low Bb is still playing sharp after the adjustment has been made, a second filing may be applied without too much risk (if you are working on a piece of low-density cane, beware of crossing the resonance-reversal point).

High-Density Effect

If there is an extra-dense area hidden in the lower part of the reed, which can also cause a sharp low Bb or sharp low register, there is nothing else to be done than take a chance by gouging a large piece of wood from somewhere in the lower blade or upper stock (even if the stock has been thinned). If this does not help, toss the reed out.[30]

❖   ❖   ❖

---

[30] *There are other possible causes of the low register playing sharp:*

   * A leaking mouthpiece bed;

   * A mouthpiece insert that extends too far down into the chamber;

   * Leaking instrument pads.

   So before attacking the shoulders of your reeds in search of a nearly perfect low Bb, be sure that the rest of your equipment is in good condition. Otherwise, extreme shoulder filing might create a bite that is much too long or having the high notes crack or cut out.

IX. PREVIEW OF THE BREAK-IN PROCESS

To begin the process, you will need a live-sounding piece of cane of the correct strength. Or a slightly stiffer piece of cane may be used that you believe will display a live sound once its excess wood is cut away. Other factors (often the grain structure and cane coloration) may be used to select reeds. But remember that a not-so-good-looking piece of cane with only moderate warping tendencies may turn out to be a better-playing reed than a great-looking piece that warps excessively. So even though the visual appearance may seem important, it should be recognized that any potentially live-sounding reed may be selected for the break-in process.

But a live-sounding piece of cane is not enough in itself to ensure success. This is because within as little as two or three minutes' playing time, the performance qualities of many reeds will begin to decline toward unacceptable levels due to the natural warping and swelling actions. When this happens, it is not advisable to begin using more and more embouchure pressure in an attempt to force the reed into submission because a distorted embouchure will serve to complicate the problem, not to cure it. Therefore, only minor concessions in the blowing style should be made while breaking in a reed. Then as the unavoidable decline in performance continues during the later minutes of the playing interval, the following conclusion will nearly always be drawn:

SINCE THERE IS NO PRACTICAL WAY TO PREVENT THE REED FROM EXPRESSING ITS NATURAL WARPING AND SWELLING ACTIONS, THE MAIN PURPOSE OF THE BREAK-IN PROCESS WILL BE TO PROVOKE THE REED INTO DISPLAYING THESE DETRIMENTAL TENDENCIES. THEN THE PROBLEMS MAY BE CORRECTED AS MUCH AS POSSIBLE BY APPLYING THE ADJUSTMENT TECHNIQUES.

The method of provoking the reed is amazingly simple. All that is needed is to play easily on the reed for a 5-minute or 10-minute interval while maintaining a natural embouchure. During this time the tone quality and other performance factors may become extremely unmusical, but the player will not be concerned with this. Rather, the player will be considering the adjustments to be made at the end of the playing interval and looking forward to the improvement in performance when the adjustments are applied.

The duration of each break-in session should be rather short, about 10 minutes' playing time followed by whatever amount of adjusting time that is needed to restore or improve the reed. And it will be found that three or four of these short sessions performed one day after another will bring the reed into a higher state of evolution than a single, hour-long session. But if it is desired to spend an hour or more a day on reed working, the time may be divided among a few reeds that are simultaneously involved in the break-in process.

As the warping and swelling tendencies of a reed are progressively reduced through a series of short break-in sessions, the reed will evolve toward a better state than when it was brand new (if not, then the reed may be tossed out). That is, you will be working with a live-sounding piece of cane that is relatively leak-free against the mouthpiece (compared to its original state) while the reed is in its dynamic shape. When it becomes apparent that the reed has withstood nearly enough dynamic balancing of its backside, more emphasis will be placed on bringing its lengthwise proportions of wood into better balance.

Quick-Cut Reeds and Fully Balanced Reeds

Quick-Cut Reeds

The exact definition for a quick-cut reed must be decided by each player according to the tools acquired and skills gained. But it is likely that the procedure will include some dynamic balancing and cutting down thick edges.

One area of agreement may be that the procedure should not take too much time away from practicing. But regardless of a conception about how much time should be spent breaking in a reed, the reed will be in greater control of the situation than the player. Some reeds may present only minor problems that can be quickly resolved while others may display more serious problems that will take extra time to repair.

When working with a quick-cut reed, there is one problem that must be recognized. The problem is that removing too much wood, especially during dynamic balancing, may weaken the reed excessively; and the tip must then be clipped to restore the reed strength. Although there is nothing wrong with a small amount of clipping, larger clips may destroy the proportions of wood in the blade. And the only way to restore the proportions is through a time-consuming rebalancing that may be beyond your present abilities to accomplish.

Fully Balanced Reeds

Fully balanced reeds represent the highest art and craft in reed adjustment, and these reeds will receive a much more extensive cutting than quick-cut reeds.

The principal difference is rather than trying to protect the reed strength, which is a requirement for quick-cut reeds, a fully balanced reed may have its backside reflattened on each of several initial break-in sessions. And the weakened reed strength may require many clippings of the tip to keep returning the blade nearly to its proper stiffness.

To maintain the correct proportions of wood in the blade during this process, the micrometer assembly and a good set of ideal measurements will be mandatory. Beginning with a half-strength-harder reed may also help to maintain stiffness. But even when these requirements are met, there are still many things that can go wrong.

CONSIDER THAT A FRAGILE PIECE OF CANE IS REPEATEDLY PLACED INTO A HOSTILE ENVIRONMENT WHERE IT IS LITERALLY BEING RIPPED APART BY THE FORCES IMPOSED UPON IT. AND AT THE SAME TIME THE PLAYER IS INSISTING THAT SOME TYPE OF SYMMETRY BE MAINTAINED THAT MAY NOT BE IN ACCORDANCE WITH THE TRUE NATURE OF THE REED. IT SHOULD BE NO WONDER THAT THE CHARACTER OF A FULLY BALANCED REED WILL BE

DRAMATICALLY CHANGED FROM WHEN IT WAS BRAND-NEW,

SOMETIMES FOR THE BETTER BUT OFTEN FOR THE WORSE.

This means that regardless of favorable first impressions, most reeds are incapable of being fully balanced. In reviewing the history of a failed reed, you may regret that the reed may have made an excellent quick-cut reed if only the cutting had not been so severe. But this type of negative thinking is extremely counterproductive. If you do not keep trying to make fully balanced reeds, then obviously you will never be successful at making them.

Significant problems. Many reeds will display a significant adjustment problem while they are engaged in the fully balanced process. If the problem cannot be satisfactorily repaired or if the reed develops a second significant problem, it may be best to toss the reed out and go to work on a new piece of cane.

Minor problems. If the significant problem can be eliminated (or better yet, if the problem never develops), the only adjustments remaining will be minor problems. These minor problems often involve the extreme tonal ranges of the instrument; specifically, the high F and low Bb.

The high-note/low-note balancing may require a sensitive adjustment, or the pitch relationship between high F and low Bb may be somehow misaligned.

Qualities of a Finished Fully Balanced Reed.

In order to achieve the fastest response and greatest dependability, the reed strength will be about equal to the embouchure strength while the embouchure is held in a comfortable, efficient manner.

The tone quality will be extremely well-centered without the sound becoming thin; the reed will play at very loud dynamic levels without the pitch going flat; the subtone low register will pop out of the instrument when using a breath attack (no tongue or very little tongue); and the high notes will not crack even though the embouchure is fairly relaxed.[31]

---

[31] *Actually, the security of the high notes may present a lingering problem. But remember that this is a fairly new reed. The fibers are still adjusting, the tip may be closing toward the mouthpiece, and a mild primary warp may still be trying to develop. These minor problems may be corrected in the near future after further observing the reed tendencies.*

Rotators and Keepers

The Water-Induced Concave Warp

As the reed receives more and more dynamic balancing, the concave warp will gain more and more power in the reed shaping. And throughout the break-in process, the 10-minute playing intervals will not expose the reed to very much water soaking.

This is an important point because when a reed is finally exposed to prolonged water soaking, the water might amplify the power of the concave warp beyond that of the dynamic balancing. And the reed might then develop a leak-producing concave warp in its dynamic shape that may be too severe to repair. The water-induced concave warp can also be very mysterious because it may have a delayed reaction. The warp may not appear for a day or more after the water exposure.

Rotators

A rotator may be defined as a reed that can be successfully alternated with the playing of other reeds (in a rotating playing order). Or it may be defined as a reed that will retain its performance qualities when it is stored off the mouthpiece for long periods of time.

The break-in process requires the simultaneous engagement of a few reeds through a series of short-play/long-rest intervals. And all reeds engaged in the process will therefore begin their lives as rotators.

Since fully balanced reeds receive many dynamic balancings during several or more short break-in sessions, these reeds will develop very powerful concave warps before they are placed into serious play. When they are finally placed into serious play, they will be much more susceptible to the water-induced concave warp than quick-cut reeds.

This means that fully balanced reeds must not be played into a pronounced water-soaked state. To avoid this state, a fully balanced reed may be played for about an hour or an hour and a half; then the reed will be stored in a box or holder while a fresh reed is brought into play. When employing the safety of this method, fully balanced reeds may be designated as rotators for their entire useful lives.

Keepers

When a quick-cut reed is finally placed into serious play, it will be designated as a keeper because it will be stored (kept) on the mouthpiece for its entire useful life even though at times it may become quite wet.[32] This is possible because quick-cut reeds receive only moderate dynamic balancing and are more resistant to the water-induced concave warp than fully balanced reeds.

Back-up reeds. The best time to make back-up reeds is when the previous keeper is about to be tossed out. But instead of making just one replacement, try to work on two or three. Any surplus quick-cut reeds produced in this manner may be stockpiled for future use.

When a stockpiled reed is about to be placed into serious play, the long period of dryness the reed has just experienced may cause additional activity in the primary warp. So one more break-in session may be needed.

Conclusions

When making fully balanced reeds, the player is constantly searching for problems so that they may be repaired. But this is not the best way to make quick-cut reeds because of the risk involved in removing too much wood.

So an attitude change might help in this area. That is, when working on a quick-cut reed, it may be better to enjoy the things that are right with the reed rather than worrying too much about what is wrong with the reed. With this attitude the risk of overcutting may be greatly lessened.

❖   ❖   ❖

---

[32] *It is also possible to use quick-cut reeds as rotators. But it may also be found that a reed will require additional dynamic balancing each time it is allowed thoroughly to dry out off the mouthpiece.*

X. THE BREAK-IN PROCESS

Assembling the Equipment

The Mouthpiece

Place the mouthpiece on the neck cork at its best-playing position and leave it there. Intonation should be corrected as much as possible by adjusting the reed, not by moving the mouthpiece in and out on the neck cork.

The Reed

Place the reed on the mouthpiece so that the edges of the reed are parallel with the edges of the mouthpiece rails. Do not offset the reed tip to one side or the other in an attempt to find a better-playing position because this will complicate the adjustment process. If the reed is to be balanced anyway, the need to offset the tip will probably disappear.

The reed tip edge, however, may be moved a bit upwardly or downwardly as a temporary adjustment to the reed strength. Moving the tip edge upwardly will increase the stiffness, and moving the tip edge downwardly will decrease the stiffness.

The Ligature

Place the ligature at its best-playing position and leave it there during the break-in process. Variations in the ligature position can change the reed response, but these variations cannot be properly evaluated until a later stage in the reed development.

The Embouchure

Remember to play easily on the reed while maintaining a nearly natural embouchure.

Breaking In a Quick-Cut Reed, Part 1

The goal in creating a quick-cut reed is to perform the necessary adjustments in a minimum of time while taking care not to remove too much wood. Many reeds will respond acceptably to quick cutting, but others may present special problems that might require additional break-in sessions to repair. In any case, if a reed is not responding properly, leave it alone or toss it out.

The following break-in process contains many details concerning common procedures. For a more concise view of the quick-cut process, see the summary on page 110.

The First Session

1. Observe the clock; then play easily on the reed for exactly 5 minutes to provoke the warping actions;

2. When the 5-minute interval has elapsed, take the reed from the mouthpiece and remove the excess water by drawing the reed between your thumb and fingers; also, wipe the mouthpiece bed and lower rails to remove any water residing there;[33]

3. Now use the straight edge, mouthpiece, and desk lamp to check the amount of crosswise and lengthwise warping of the reed back as discussed on page 13; the amount of warping observed will determine the amount of cutting needed to reflatten the back;

4. Apply enough cutting strokes to the backside to close the edge gaps; the recommended cutting procedure is to rough cut with the reed knife, fine finish with the sandpaper plate, then polish finish with the mill file; if you have not acquired all these tools, use whatever you have to dynamically balance the reed backside;

---

[33] *The simple act of removing the excess water will in itself add resonance to the sound and snap to the articulations when the reed is returned to the mouthpiece. Do not mistake this effect for any result of cutting the reed. No matter, a nearly new reed will quickly dull and delay when it again becomes loaded with too much water.*

5. Test play the reed for a few seconds to evaluate its present state of development; if the reed seems to be evolving correctly, go on to Step 6; but if either of the two following exceptions is observed, the playing interval of this break-in session may be ended;

Exception 1: The reed is displaying a significant adjustment problem (an upper-blade primary warp, extremely weak strength, or any of the various other problems); at this time the upper blade may be recut to its proper specifications and the special problems at least partially repaired—the first break-in session is now ended;

Exception 2: An extremely large amount of wood was removed during the first cutting of the primary warp; this reed may be in danger of being overcut and may be displaying temporary performance qualities that are not really reflective of its true nature—the first break-in session is now ended;

6. Observe the clock; then play easily on the reed for another 5-minute interval (total playing time will then be 10 minutes) to provoke the warping actions further;

7. Dry the reed, check the back for warping, and reflatten the backside again (if needed—it often is);

8. Recut the upper blade to its proper specifications; then test play the reed to determine its present state of performance;

9. Additional time may now be spent to evolve the reed; such as, clipping the tip, thinning the lower blade, etc.; and

10. Make any appropriate comments or corrections on the reed abstract.

The Second Session

While the reed is still in its static shape, the backside shaping may be examined to discover any potential problems. These checks should be made after the upper blade has been moistened and the wrinkles pressed out of the tip but before any notes are played on the reed.

Upper-blade primary warp. Use the straight edge and desk lamp to check for a primary warp in the upper part of the blade. If the warp is found, do not cut it at this time. Instead, wait until the reed has been test played to determine if the warp is actually causing a performance problem.

Concaving and arching. These items, as discussed on page 125, are usually associated with fully balanced reeds because of the greater amount of backside cutting that fully balanced reeds receive. But since certain quick-cut reeds might also be improved by applying the adjustment techniques, these items are being previewed now as a supplement to the quick-cutting process.

The straight edge and desk lamp are also used to check the amount of crosswise concaving in the lower blade and stock (where wood was removed during the primary-warp cutting in the previous session) while the reed is still in its static shape. But if the static-shape concave warp appears to be too deep, do not cut it at this time. Wait until the reed has been test played to see if the warp is actually causing a performance problem (sometimes even a small amount of concaving can cause a problem, which is why this item may be important for a quick-cut reed).

Next, use the mouthpiece and desk lamp to examine the amount of arching in the stock while the reed is still in its static shape. But once again, do not cut away any excess arching until the reed has been test played.

Quick dynamic shape. The reason why the reed must not be played before making the preceding checks is because certain reeds will modulate into their dynamic shapes within a few seconds of being placed into vibration. If this happens to the project reed, the opportunity to examine and adjust the reed in its static shape may be lost until the reed has been rested again.

This also means that the playing test might be very short, perhaps only a half-dozen notes, to prevent the reed from modulating too far into its dynamic shape.

Playing test. As the first few notes are played during this test, be prepared to make a quick decision about any adjustments in the reed static shape. For example, if the upper blade is producing a clouded tone, there may be swelling in the tip area or the primary warp may be too severe. For another example, if the reed has "stiffened" overnight or has lost too much of its resonance (compared to the way it was playing during its last break-in session), then the concave warp may need cutting. Finally, when a reed is played during its static shape, its tip will be closed up toward the mouthpiece; this will make the strength feel weak (the effect will disappear as the reed reaches its dynamic shape). But if the reed feels unacceptably weak, the tip may be clipped or the arching in the stock may be cut while the reed is still in its static shape.

After the preliminary checks and adjustments, the reed will be ready for its second break-in session:

1. The first 5-minute playing interval and subsequent dynamic balancing are performed in the same fashion as during the first break-in session; and if the two exceptions on page 107 are not found, proceed to the second 5-minute playing interval;

2. The second 5-minute playing interval and subsequent adjustments are also performed as during the first break-in session with one possible exclusion; the exclusion is that if the reed strength is becoming too weak from too much cutting of the backside, repair of the primary warp may be reduced or omitted; and

3. Make any appropriate comments or corrections on the reed abstract.

Accelerating the Part 1 Process

After some experience has been gained, the Part 1 process may be accelerated by the following methods:

The playing time of the very first playing session may be extended to 20 minutes (four 5-minute intervals) provided that no significant problems develop or that the strength does not become too weak through overcutting the primary warp. The playing time of all subsequent Part 1 sessions, though, should not exceed 10 minutes as previously described.

Also, since a reed requires only a few hours to regain its full static shape, a reed may be adjusted in both the morning and evening of the same day.

Finally, if it seems appropriate to do so, the second break-in session may be skipped.

Breaking In a Quick-Cut Reed, Part 2

If all has gone well and one or two back-up reeds have been similarly prepared, the quick-cut reed may be ready for more extended play.

The Part 2 process begins with yet another 10-minute playing interval followed by subsequent adjustments (with the possible exclusion of cutting the primary warp). But this time, after the adjustments have been made, the reed is returned to the mouthpiece for an hour or more to provide its first experience in prolonged playing while becoming thoroughly wetted. The performance characteristics are bound to change during this long session, and more adjustments may be made either during the session or at the session end. However, try not to cut the primary warp during the later part of the session.[34]

Since a quick-cut reed is likely to be designated as a keeper, the reed may now be stored on the mouthpiece for its entire useful life.

Table 12

SUMMARY: BREAKING IN A QUICK-CUT REED

Part 1

The First Session

1. Play the reed for 5 minutes;

2. Reflatten the backside;

3. Play the reed for another 5 minutes;

4. Reflatten the backside again;

5. Remove the upper-blade swelling; and

6. Make other adjustments.

---

[34] *Cutting the advanced primary warp is a separate topic presented on page 114.*

The Second Session

Same as the first session; and

Beware of removing too much wood from the back.

Part 2

The Single Session

1. Repeat the second session;

2. Keep playing the reed for an hour or more;

3. Make adjustments but try not to cut the primary warp during the later part of the session; and

4. Store the keeper on the mouthpiece.

Breaking In a Fully Balanced Reed, Part 1

The break-in process for a fully balanced reed is an elaboration of that for a quick-cut reed. The goal in creating a fully balanced reed is to minimize every detriment that the reed displays, and this may take a great deal of time and patience. Most reeds are not capable of being fully balanced, but the only sure way to determine which reeds will be successful is to continue to cut and try them until a fully balanced reed has been produced.

The following break-in process contains many references to the material just described for a quick-cut reed. For a more concise view of the fully balanced process, see the summary on page 113.

The First Session

The first session is performed in the same manner as a quick-cut reed. If desired, the first session may be extended to 20 minutes' playing time (four 5-minute intervals).

The Second Session

On the second session the preliminary checks and adjustments should be made (review pages 107 and 108) and the playing time limited to two 5-minute intervals. A fully balanced reed will have its backside completely reflattened at the end of the second interval even though this might require a large clipping of the tip and near-complete recutting of the blade (the micrometer assembly will be mandatory for this type of recutting).

Abandoning the Project

At the end of the second session (or sometime in the near future), the player may decide that the reed is incapable of becoming fully balanced. This reed may be declared a quick-cut reed or may be tossed out.

Subsequent Sessions

Keep playing and adjusting the reed through the 10-minute sessions until the primary warp no longer appears at the 10-minute mark. To consider Part 1 to be finished, though, all significant problems must be nearly minimized; and the tone, strength, and intonation must be generally correct. In order to reach this state (a near state of equilibrium) it would not be unusual for the reed to have experienced a half-dozen break-in sessions; and some more difficult reeds might require a dozen or more sessions (oppositely, occasional reeds might evolve through the Part 1 sessions in less time). The number of sessions is not the important point, however. The important point is that you keep working at the reed as long as you feel it is developing positively.

Accelerating the Part 1 Process

If a few reeds are being simultaneously adjusted, then one of these reeds may be designated as an accelerator and adjusted in both the morning and evening of each day, thus halving the number of days required to enter the Part 2 process. Also, with even more experience you will discover that certain reeds may be advanced to the Part 2 process even though their backsides still require some reflattening at the 10-minute mark.

Breaking In a Fully Balanced Reed, Part 2

If all has gone well, the fully balanced reed is now ready for more extended play.

The Part 2 process is a single, one-hour-long interval that introduces the reed to prolonged playing while becoming thoroughly wetted. The performance characteristics are bound to change during this long session, and more adjustments may be made either during the session or at the session end (or if you choose, these adjustments may be delayed until the next day). But try not to cut the primary warp during the later part of the session (once again, see page 114).

Unlike a quick-cut reed, a fully balanced reed is likely to be designated as a rotator. And the fully balanced rotator will now be returned to a stack or box to await the Part 3 process.

Breaking In a Fully Balanced Reed, Part 3

Keep repeating the Part 1 sessions until the primary warp no longer appears at the 10-minute mark or until it is otherwise determined that the reed is ready for performance.

Table 13

SUMMARY: BREAKING IN A FULLY BALANCED REED

Part 1

Session 1

    1. Play the reed for 5 minutes;

    2. Reflatten the backside;

    3. Play the reed for another 5 minutes;

Continued on page 114

4. Reflatten the backside again;

5. Remove the upper-blade swelling; and

6. Make other adjustments.

Subsequent Sessions

Keep repeating Session 1 until the primary warp no longer appears at the 10-minute mark or until you otherwise decide to advance the reed to the Part 2 process.

Part 2

The Single Session

1. Play the reed for one hour;

2. Make adjustments but try not to cut the primary warp during the later part of the session; and

3. Return the rotator to the stack or box.

Part 3

All Sessions

Keep repeating Part 1 until the primary warp no longer appears at the 10-minute mark or until you otherwise decide that the reed is ready for performance.

Cutting the Advanced Primary Warp

In the break-in processes just described for quick-cut reeds and fully balanced reeds, it is recommended not to cut the primary warp during the later minutes of the hour-long (Part 2) sessions. This recommendation is made for two reasons. The first reason is that allowing a bit of extra wood to remain in the primary warp will serve to protect against a possible water-induced concave warp. The second reason is to ensure that the reed will retain enough strength so that the hour-long session will actually be

114

completed (completing the session will develop the vibration expansion, and removing the advanced expansion will help to stabilize the reed and finish the break-in process).

Nonetheless, many reeds will display excess primary warping during the later part of the long session. If the problem becomes too severe or if it appears that this is to be a permanently unacceptable condition in the reed, go ahead and cut the warp and accept any consequences as part of the nature of the reed. This cutting might be applied at the 20-minute mark, the 40-minute mark, or the 60-minute mark; but hopefully, not all three marks.

It may also be found that a newer reed might continue to develop a trouble-causing primary warp during its first few performance sessions (this is especially true for a rotator that has thoroughly dried out off the mouthpiece). It may then be necessary to place the reed through a long practice session with the specific goal of repairing the primary warp during the later minutes of the session.

❖   ❖   ❖

115

XI. ADDITIONAL ADJUSTMENTS

Cane Density

The cane density determines how stiffly a reed will play once it has been cut to a set of ideal measurements. Specifically, lower density cane will result in reeds of weaker strengths, and higher density cane will result in reeds of stiffer strengths.

After they have been manufactured, reeds are factory graded on a spring-tension gauge and sorted into boxes graduated in half-strengths. But because of inconsistencies in the automatic-cutting process and subtle variations in the cane densities, each box of reeds will contain reeds of slightly different strengths.

General Effects

Players using low-density cane (Nos. 1 1/2 and 2) will often need to make reeds thicker than their ideal measurements.

Players using medium-density cane (Nos. 2 1/2, 3, and 3 1/2) will have the greatest success at maintaining their ideal measurements but will sometimes need to make reeds that are thicker or thinner. Maintaining the ideal measurements for the upper blade is the most desirable technique because the tone and response will be closely matched from reed to reed, and minor differences in strength and pitch can be adjusted by changing the mass of wood in the lower blade.

Players using high-density cane (Nos. 4 and 5) may find that acquiring satisfactory reeds is largely a matter of luck. Although a player may develop a set of ideal measurements for these reeds, many of the reeds may require thinner cuts. But even so, the thinner cuts may still be unsatisfactory.[35]

Specific Effects

Each player will develop a preference for a particular brand and strength of reeds. But within a box of these reeds, the player must further sort the reeds into subclassifications of low density, medium density, and high density (or weak, medium, and stiff). The specific effects for a particular boxed strength are similar to the general effects previously described for reeds of all strengths, but they are being classified on a much finer scale.

Low density. Since this cane is quite weak, the reed may remain slightly thicker than your ideal measurements. But some cutting is usually necessary.

Low-density reeds may serve some utilitarian purposes, but they are seldom suitable for virtuoso performances on the alto and soprano saxes (although there may be exceptions to this observation).

Medium density. Reeds that are nearly the correct strength may receive a straightforward adjustment. These reeds may be cut to your ideal measurements to see exactly how the density is being expressed. Then fine-tuning adjustments may be applied by the empirical method.

---

[35] *The instrument voice also plays an important role in the selection of the reed strength.*

Tenor and baritone saxes can be successfully played using reeds ranging from No. 1 1/2 to No. 5, the strength depending on compatibility with the mouthpiece and embouchure. One reason for this wide range of usable strengths is the large bore sizes of these saxophones. The greater volume of vibrating air (free vibrations) in the large bore will keep the vibrating and resonating actions of the reeds under greater control even though the reeds may be very weak or very stiff. Another reason is that reeds for lower pitched instruments are not required to vibrate at the rapid frequencies of the smaller saxes, so less physical demand is placed on tenor and baritone reeds.

Soprano and alto reeds, however, are required to vibrate at much higher frequency rates. And being less controlled by the smaller instrument bores, weaker reeds like Nos. 1 1/2 and 2 may be subject to wildness in the tone/strength/intonation force group. But even if the wildness is not found, these reeds may have short lifetimes because of the rapid vibration frequencies imparted to the weak cane. Oppositely, extra-dense cane for the soprano and alto may be too resistant to the controlling influence of the more limited free vibrations in the small instrument bores; and the embouchure may be too weak to match the toughness of the cane.

<u>High density</u>. Since high-density cane contains too much damping material, the front side of the stock may be thinned to increase the resonance. And thinning the reed tip or tip edge by one-half thousandth of an inch is a relatively safe adjustment.

The next modification to be tried might be to thin the upper heart to clear the tone quality. But even if this technique works, the pitch may begin to go flat after some playing time has been gained. So the reed must be clipped to rethicken the upper heart and raise the pitch, and you will be back nearly to where you started.

Another adjustment to be tried is to remove some wood from the lower blade to reduce the reed strength. But another problem might then be revealed. It is sometimes possible to remove extreme amounts of wood from the lower blade or to lower the shoulder edge by an exceptional distance, all with little effect on the reed performance. What has happened in these instances is that the pivot point is not located at the shoulder edge at all. Instead, the point is suspended somewhere nearer to the bite line; and the reed is essentially functioning without a lower blade.

Diagnostic Reed Clipping

The reed clipper may be used to solve a variety of problems. When the clipping is restricted to removing very small amounts of wood from the tip edge, these adjustments will usually be successful. There will be times, though, when even the smallest clips will result in the impairment of the reed rather than in its improvement.

Lost Resonance

Although attention may be given to increasing the thickness of a particular reed area, the entire contour of the blade may become too thick. And this extra wood can contribute to unnecessary damping and bending resistance.

First, check the tip edge on the profiling tool. Next, use the micrometer assembly to check the entire surface of the blade and remove any specks of extra wood. Then examine the thickness and taper of the side rails for bumps or high spots. Also, test the reed for a sharp low Bb and file the shoulder edge if needed.

The Illusion of the Reed Tip

If the player is unaware of this problem, the reed might be completely impaired by one or two small clips.

This problem can usually be avoided simply by measuring the tip edge, reed tip, and heart tip (or by measuring the entire upper blade).

Relocation of an Upper-Blade Primary Warp

When a reed is clipped, an upper-blade primary warp may be moved closer to the tip edge. And now being located in a more highly active area of the reed, the warp may cause more trouble than before the clipping.

Relocation of Hidden Hard Spots

Hidden hard spots will also be moved upwardly into the more active areas of the reed.

Actually, this effect can be a benefit if the reed was clipped to increase its strength. But if the clipping was to resolve some other detriment, the reed strength may now be much stiffer than expected by the small clip.

Intonation Reversal

A rare occasion will find a reed that is playing too stiffly yet the pitch is slightly flat. And if this reed is clipped to raise its pitch, the player may be amazed to find that the resulting pitch is even flatter than before the clip.

The problem in this situation concerns a very hard area somewhere in the lower blade (even though the upper blade is performing correctly). And the lower blade is overpowering the embouchure to such an extent that it is physically impossible to lip the tones up to the correct pitch. If this reed is clipped, the lower blade will further overpower the embouchure; and the situation will become even worse.

The solution to this unusual problem is an exact reversal of the general rule of adjusting intonation. That is, this reed should not be clipped any more to raise its pitch.

Instead, the lower blade should be thinned. Then it may be found that the tones will sharpen up to pitch as the lower-blade strength and embouchure strength are brought into a closer state of balance.

If too much wood is removed, however, the embouchure may begin to overpower the reed; and the pitch may then begin to go flat in accordance with the general rule of intonation adjustment.

How To Clip a Reed With Minimum Risk

If you are adjusting a reed with only average performance qualities, the reed may be clipped in a straightforward manner. And if something goes wrong, the reed may be tossed out with no great loss. But if you are working on a favorite reed or an excellent piece of cane, an extra-cautious approach will ensure that any complications will be held to a minimum effect.

When applying an extra-cautious approach, the procedure is to remove any unnecessary wood before the clip is actually made. And this procedure may seem contrary to your instincts. That is, an already-too-weak reed may be made even weaker before it is ready to be clipped.

Table 14

CLIPPING A REED WITH MINIMUM RISK

1. Check the back for air leaks and remove any that are found; the restored compression will give a much better estimation of the true strength of the reed;

2. Measure the entire upper blade and remove any specks of extra wood; these seemingly insignificant bits of wood are only clouding the tone quality and giving a false impression of the true character of the reed;

3. If you have been neglecting the lower blade, now is a good time to bring it into the proper shape;

   But if you decide that the lower blade is all right, measure the intersections nearest the reed shoulder and mark those measurements on

Continued on page 122

121

the abstract (in case something goes wrong with the soon-to-be-thicker shoulder, you can recut the lower blade back to its previous measurements);

4. Begin clipping the tip by very small amounts until the reed is satisfactory or until a slight clouding of the tone develops; if the clouding actually develops, return to Step No. 2; and

5. Measure and cut the blade one more time.

The Relative Intonation of High F and Low Bb

If the high F and low Bb are in tune with each other, then the scales and intervals lying between those two notes should also be in tune.

Table 15 shows the conditions and problems that can alter the pitch of these two notes. Adjusting one of these problems can result in another of the conditions. Keep correcting the problems until the relative intonation is satisfactory.

The Pop Test

This is a visual/action test that helps determine how well the reed is seating on the mouthpiece.

First, either the thumb or ligature is used to hold the reed on the mouthpiece. Next, the mouthpiece barrel is plugged by the palm or finger. Then the air is sucked out of the mouthpiece.

If a reed passes this test, it will stick to the mouthpiece rails for a short while. And when the air pressure suddenly equalizes, the reed will make a solid popping sound as it springs away from the mouthpiece rails. Oppositely, a reed that will not stick to the rails or springs open with a dull thud will have failed the test.

It might be assumed that the primary warp will hold the reed away from the mouthpiece rails and cause the reed to fail the test. But this is not always so. You will find many reeds with moderate primary warps that pass the pop test with ease, and you will also find reeds with very flat backsides that will not pass the test. So before

Table 15

ADJUSTING THE RELATIVE INTONATION OF HIGH F AND LOW Bb

Condition	Problem
1. F = sharp and Bb = sharp	a. Leaking backside; b. Too much wood in the blade; or c. Upper-blade primary warp
2. F = sharp and Bb = in tune	Same as above
3. F = flat and Bb = in tune	a. Tip bent toward mouthpiece; b. Upper-blade primary warp; c. Tip needs clipping; or d. Stock is arched
4. F = in tune and Bb = sharp	a. Upper-blade primary warp; b. Extremely stiff lower blade; or c. Shoulder needs filing (if the entire low register is sharp, the tip may be too thick); and
5. F = flat and Bb = sharp	a. Tip bent toward mouthpiece; b. Upper-blade primary warp; or c. Too much wood in the front side of the stock

attacking the primary warp, it is better to examine the shape of the side rails and to measure the edge lines with the micrometer.

If some area of the side rails or edge lines is too thick, the thick area may function as a stress riser that prevents the reed from bending evenly along the mouthpiece rail, thereby creating an air leak. Also, if one side rail or edge line is too much thicker than the other (particularly, in the lower blade), the left-side/right-side imbalance can cause the reed to twist; and the thicker side of the blade will not achieve an air seal.

In another instance the shoulder or lower blade may be too strong to allow the reed to bend along the mouthpiece facing. Cutting the primary warp may help to resolve this situation.

Other conditions will also be found. Extra-thin or extra-thick tips and upper corners, split tips, and pronounced upper-blade primary warps may cause reeds to fail the test. But it may be doubtful whether the pop test is valid in these cases.

Expansion and Contraction

Vibration Expansion

This is the most common cause of expansion in the blade. As certain fibers lose part of their elasticity during vibration (disintegration), they will no longer be able to contract back to their original shapes. Therefore, vibration expansion is a permanent condition that will not cure itself when the reed is dried and rested.

The expanded areas can create stress risers and excess water absorption that will distort the tone and slow the response of the reed. So the expanded areas must be thinned down to your ideal measurements to restore the reed performance.

Water-Absorption Expansion

It might seem that a reed may expand like a sponge when it is soaked in water, but this is not usually true. Instead, the surprising effect of water-absorption expansion is that the reed areas will not become thicker until the reed begins to dry out. This is often a temporary condition (the expanded areas may return nearly to their previous shapes when the reed is thoroughly dried and rested).[36]

When water-absorption expansion occurs, it can cause a complication in the adjustment process. That is, the damp blade may be cut to remove the vibration expansion. But then the drier blade might need cutting once again to remove the water-absorption expansion. Test play the now-drier reed before cutting the thick areas. A stiff reed may receive the extra cutting, but a weak reed may not require the extra cutting.

Heat Expansion

Heat expansion is rarely a factor in reed adjustment.

Contraction

Certain areas of the fibers might begin to contract when they are wetted and vibrated, and this is usually a permanent condition. If some reed areas become too thin through contraction, the situation must be endured until the reed is ready to be clipped.

Reworking the Lower Areas

Cutting an Arched Stock

Description. The stock has developed a lengthwise curve wherein the shoulder and heel are touching the mouthpiece bed, but the area between the shoulder and heel is suspended away from the mouthpiece bed (the arching might also extend into the lower blade).

Symptoms. The reed tip will close up toward the mouthpiece, the high F may play flat or cut out, or there may be a severe weakening of the tone quality (the weakened tone is similar to that of a pocket warp).

---

[36] *If you try the experiment in Footnote 4 on page 21, you will find that reeds usually become much wider rather than much thicker when they are water soaked.*

<u>Causes</u>. Although this warp may be a natural occurrence, it is usually a result of cutting the primary and tangent warps. There are two special conditions, however, that must be understood.

The first condition is to realize that an arched-stock curve is the exact opposite of a tangent-warp curve, and a paradox may be found. That is, cutting a dynamic-shape tangent warp may result in a static-shape arch; and cutting the static-shape arch may renew the dynamic-shape tangent warp. Therefore, some compromise in the cutting may be needed.

The second condition concerns polishing the backside on the flat mill file. Since the file polishing might in itself cause the arching (in an "allergic" reaction), the file must be abandoned when working on that particular reed.[37] To be sure that this condition will be well-remembered, write "archer no file" on the reed abstract (as shown on page 42); and it would be a good idea to write "arch" on the reed stock.

Illustration 41

TIP-EDGE VIEW: CHECKING FOR AN ARCHED STOCK

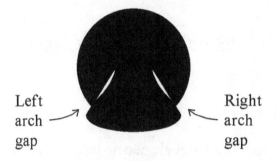

Left
arch
gap

Right
arch
gap

Look through the tip opening down into the mouthpiece; the reed/mouthpiece assembly may be pivoted to the left and right to view each gap separately; also, a pronounced concave warp may show a third light-beam arch gap at the stock end (not illustrated)

<u>Checking for an arched stock</u>. The reed, mouthpiece, and desk lamp are used in the same manner as when checking the lower-blade edge gaps. But peer deeper into the mouthpiece to view the stock arch gaps. Another problem may then arise, and that

---

[37] *The "allergic" effect might also be found when polishing the back on a piece of No. 600 sandpaper, in which case that technique must also be abandoned for that particular reed.*

Illustration 42

CUTTING AN ARCHED STOCK

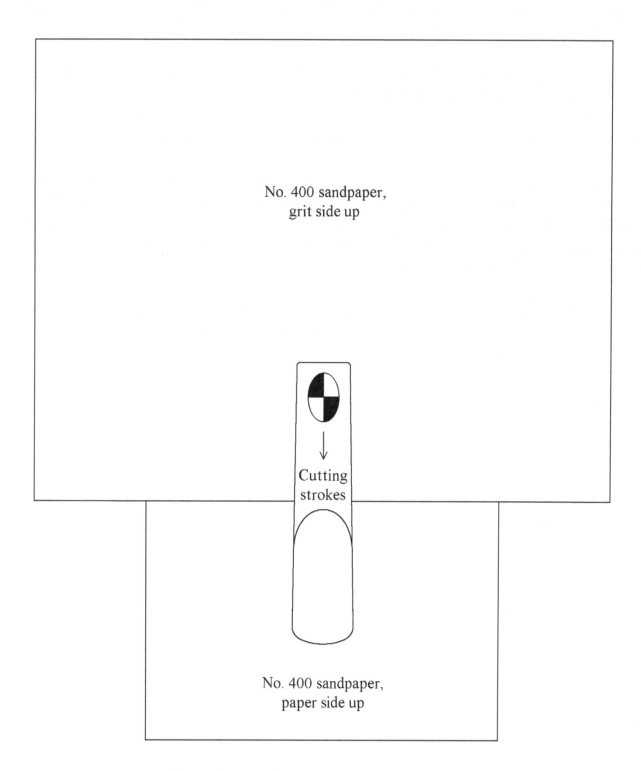

No. 400 sandpaper,
grit side up

Cutting
strokes

No. 400 sandpaper,
paper side up

This cutting may be centered or offset to one side;
when in doubt, use the centered-cutting technique

127

problem concerns gravity. If the mouthpiece is too heavy, its weight might flatten out the arch gaps so that they cannot be seen. So if you are using a metal mouthpiece or some other piece of heavy equipment, the reed/mouthpiece assembly might be held upside down when viewed into the lamp. Or a lighter mouthpiece may be used to make the check in the right-side-up position.

How to cut the arch. The lower part of the stock backside may be sanded on the surface plate as shown in Illustration 42. The small piece of sandpaper is used to keep the reed level, but it is placed paper side up to prevent its cutting into the wood (this is the same small piece of sandpaper that is used to shape the tip edge).

How much wood to remove in the static shape. Because this adjustment may cause additional activity in the primary warp, do not make any more than 10 or 20 sanding strokes in the static shape of any one break-in session. Then as the reed continues to evolve, you may or may not decide to cut some more wood during the static shape of the next break-in session.

How much wood to remove in the dynamic shape. When the arching develops in the dynamic shape, it is best to remove the entire warp at once.

Cutting a Static-Shape Concave Warp

Condition. The reed has returned to its full static shape and is ready for its next break-in session. Most often a quick test playing (just a very few notes) will not reveal any problems. But sometimes the following two symptoms will appear. These symptoms are most likely to be found in a reed that has received extensive dynamic balancing.

Symptom 1: increased blowing resistance. The deep cupping of the concave warp is causing the lower heart to vibrate at a steeper angle (relative to the mouthpiece bed and facing) than the outer sections.

Symptom 2: lost resonance. The grain structure of the backside center section has been sheared off at too great an angle, which can cause uneven vibrating actions. Cutting the static-shape concave warp will nearly reparallel the lengthwise shear angles of the center and outer sections. And this will restore some of the lost resonance.[38]

---

[38] *Whether this adjustment is applied to correct either the blowing-resistance symptom or the lost-resonance symptom, sanding the concave warp will thin the lower side rails. And thinner side rails in themselves will probably increase the resonance.*

How to cut the warp. The static-shape concave warp is sanded on the surface plate with the finger pressure located at the reed shoulder followed by a light polishing on the mill file. Check the thickness of the lower side rails before cutting. You may decide to offset the finger pressure toward the thicker side rail to produce a more balanced left/right shape.

How much wood to remove. Although it is possible to remove the warp a small bit at a time (which will require more break-in sessions), it might be easier to apply a maximum of 30 sanding strokes all at one time. And the possible destruction of the reed will then be accepted as a willing risk.

How the primary warp is affected. Most often the primary warp will gain increased activity that will require additional dynamic balancings.

Illustration 43

BACK VIEW: SEQUENTIAL SANDING/FILING AREAS DURING
THE CUTTING OF A STATIC-SHAPE CONCAVE WARP

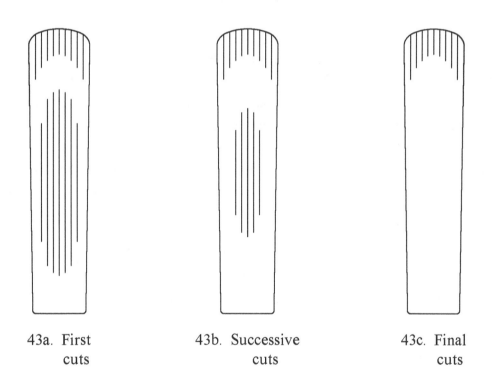

43a. First
cuts

43b. Successive
cuts

43c. Final
cuts

The Two-Beam and Three-Beam Theories

The information in this section may be viewed as a guide to repair certain conditions in a reed. But just as importantly, these theories explain why some problems cannot be reconciled.

The Two-Beam Theory

The left-side/right-side blowing test. If the reed is not responding to adjustments in the way that you would prefer, try this test.

First, assume that the blade is comprised of two lengthwise beams as shown in Illustration 44a. Next, test the tone and pitch of the middle and high Fs while blowing on only the left-side beam. Then repeat the test for the right-side beam to compare the two sides.

It may be found, for example, that the left side is playing sharp with a live sound while the right side is playing flat with a dull sound. It may also be found that the right-side high F is cutting out.

The reason why this might happen is that the left and right sides operate as separate blades even though they are connected (remember that the two sides are always vibrating in opposite directions as shown on page 71). And the aspects of interdependence also function separately for each side of the blade.

Solution 1. If the above problem is not too severe, more supporting material may be added to the lower beam on the dull-sounding side, which is accomplished by clipping the reed tip.

Solution 2. For a more severe problem, the dull-sounding edge of the reed may be sanded (hold the reed at a 90-degree angle to the surface plate while grasping the reed near its shoulder). This will remove some of the "dead" wood and will move the heart toward that edge for even more support.

The Three-Beam Theory

The blade can also be divided into three lengthwise beams as shown in Illustration 44b. This will help to understand what can happen if a reed requires too much dynamic balancing.

When the lower-blade part of the center beam is too deeply cut, the upper part of the center beam will severely overpower it. This condition will impair the performance even though the outer beams are functioning correctly.[39]

Solution. This problem will require a more extensive clipping and rebalancing than that of a normal reed, or the reed might be tossed out.

Illustration 44

THE TWO-BEAM AND THREE-BEAM THEORIES

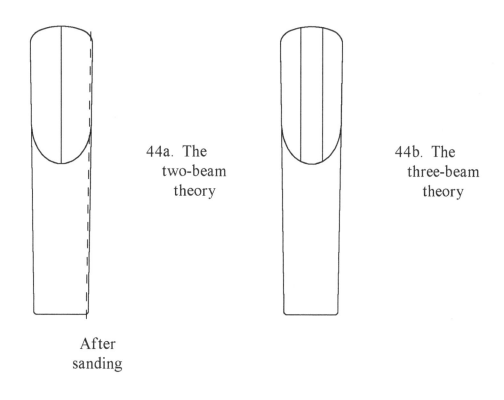

44a. The
two-beam
theory

44b. The
three-beam
theory

After
sanding

❖   ❖   ❖

---

[39] *The lower-blade centerline for a micrometer-method abstract may become thoroughly riddled with double minus signs and triple minus signs to mark the extra-thin areas.*

XII. THE REED LIFETIME

The Break-In Period

A fully balanced reed will receive most of its adjustment during the break-in period. But further refinements will be needed as its lifetime progresses.

Oppositely, a quick-cut reed receives only partial adjustment during the break-in period. So the later adjustments may be more complex than for a fully balanced reed.

There is one way, however, to reduce the complexity of the later adjustments in the lifetime of a quick-cut reed. That way is to increase the number of break-in sessions and to begin using the micrometer method for the reed tip and upper edges.

The Middle Life

The refinements to be expected for either a quick-cut reed or a fully balanced reed include resetting the upper-blade angle, further reduction of the primary warp, clipping the tip to maintain stiffness, and searching for additional expansion.

How To Manage Rotators

After a rotator has experienced a performance session, it should be checked and readjusted on the following day (sometimes the follow-up session can be skipped).

To perform the follow-up session, the reed is played for 5 or 10 minutes to bring it into its dynamic shape. Then the usual checks and adjustments may be made.

Occasionally, a presumed-short checking/adjustment session might reveal a serious problem. If it is inconvenient to begin major repairs at that time, return the reed to the break-in stack for future adjustment.

Preventing excess dryness. Try to play each rotator in the working supply for at least 10 minutes every week.

How To Manage Keepers

Another method to reduce the complexity of adjustments in the middle life of a quick-cut keeper is to disregard the problems as much as is it may be practical to do so. This attitude can be very effective when the problems involve left-side/right-side imbalance or a slightly thick tone because the reed performance may improve as the fibers are more thoroughly broken in.

Problems with air leaks and weak strength, though, may require removing the keeper from the mouthpiece for adjustment. After the repair is made, the reed should be immediately played for a while to renew the cane/mouthpiece mating and to prevent the reed from becoming too dry.

The Middle Life to the End Life

As playing hours are gained, the reed strength will gradually decline. For a compensation in the weakened cane, the upper blade may need to become thicker. (Increasing the lower-blade mass will usually serve to strengthen the reed for quite a while in its life, but a thick lower blade may become a hindrance as the reed becomes more well-used.) To accomplish the upper-blade thickening, the advanced vibration expansion may be allowed to remain; or the tip may be clipped to produce the same effect. The thicker upper blade might feel unusual to the embouchure, and the extra water weight may slow the response. But the reed may nevertheless perform quite well.[40]

At this time the reed performance may still be maintained by minor refinements. But eventually, the reed is going to become extremely sensitive to any adjustments at all. This sensitivity will be partly based on the weakening effect of removing more wood. It will also be partly based on the fact that the reed fibers have been accustomed to vibrating together in their current configuration (when more wood is removed, the redistribution of vibration stresses will further weaken some of the remaining fibers).

---

[40] *If the micrometer method is being used, + signs (plus signs) may now be coded on the abstract to mark the thick areas; or thicker upper-blade curves may be plotted that closely resemble the actual measurements of the reed. But depending on the player's temperament, it might be easier to begin using the empirical method instead of the micrometer method for the upper blade.*

Dynamic Balancing

When a reed is brand new, it might withstand the massive removal of backside wood with only a moderate reduction in stiffness. But this will no longer be true for a well-used reed.

In a well-used reed, it may be found that only a few cutting strokes on the No. 400 sandpaper might reduce the stiffness by one-eighth strength. So as the reed gains more and more age, it may become wise to test play the reed after every 1 or 2 sanding strokes so that it is not weakened any more than absolutely necessary to maintain a reasonable air seal.

Furthermore, even a small amount of dynamic balancing can move the reed tip closer to the mouthpiece tip. And since the weakened fibers may be less able to maintain an upper-blade-angle reset, this is another reason why dynamic balancing becomes increasingly more dangerous as the reed gradually progresses toward its end life.

Another method is available that offers more safety in late-life dynamic balancing. In this method the sandpaper plate is abandoned altogether. Instead, the warp lower area is lightly knifed on the clipboard; then the backside may then receive a few polishing strokes on the mill file to reblend the stock and lower blade (the reblending is optional). In using the knife technique, the air leak will be reduced without the extra upper-blade thinning that the sandpaper technique produces.

Texture Changes

The front-side blade surface will slowly transform into a powder-like coating that offers very little resistance to the knife, and at the same time the grains beneath the coating may be turning into pulp.

When this condition develops, cutting with the reed knife may remove far too much wood from the upper blade. This indicates a change to an alternate cutting tool. If you are accustomed to using the reed knife, the fine-tooth needle file may be the most comfortable. But whatever tool you select, it will not be as accurate as the knife when using the micrometer method. So it may be more convenient to begin using the empirical method for the upper blade (although the micrometer may still be used to check the general upper-blade shaping, and the knife and micrometer method may still be best for the lower blade).

The Lower Blade

Even though the upper blade is being reinforced by adding more mass, it is still wearing out at a faster rate than the lower blade. And to rebalance the lengthwise proportions of wood, mass must now be removed from the lower blade even though its strength will be reduced as a result.

This can be a strange effect. During its early life the lower blade may be thickened to increase its strength. But in its later life it may be thinned to reduce its strength.

Notice that this is the opposite of the upper-blade effect. The upper blade will begin its life as being thin. But in its later life it will become thicker.

The Flat-Pitch Paradox

The reed is playing flat and is clipped to raise its pitch. But then the low notes will not play, so the lower areas are cut to repair that problem. And now the pitch has become flat again.

This cycle is a paradox because repairing the original problem will result in the other, and repairing the other will result in the original. This cycle may be repeated again and again with the same unfortunate results. The lifetime of the reed has now ended.

❖   ❖   ❖

XIII. HAND MADE REEDS

Reeds for the smaller saxophones, the soprano and alto, have a problem when undergoing the fully balanced process. That is, the massive amount of wood removed when cutting the primary warp and subsequent clippings of the tip might result in a reed that is so short and thin that the ligature may not be able to hold it on the mouthpiece. Or even if the ligature problem does not develop, it is possible that the resonance-reversal point will be unintentionally crossed, particularly when working on a soft piece of cane.

The solution to this problem is to begin working on a reed designed for a larger instrument. For example, an alto reed may be cut from a tenor reed or a baritone reed. As the work progresses, the excess wood will be slowly eliminated until the finished reed will be the correct size.

Which Cane To Use

Begin work with your favorite brand and strength but designed for a larger instrument. Save experiments with other brands and strengths for later.

Thinning the Stock

This operation will probably be mandatory to remove the damping effect created by the excessively thick stock. Begin work before the first break-in session to minimize the primary warp. Continue to remove wood during every break-in session until the finished reed has a stock of the correct thickness. It is also best to create a stock that mildly tapers toward a thicker heel.

Removing Excess Width

The excess wood hanging over the edges of the mouthpiece rails is nothing but dead weight. It steals energy from the breath during vibration and must be removed to achieve maximum efficiency.

The left-side/right-side blowing test will be used during each break-in session to determine which side of the reed to sand or if the sanding must be equally applied to both sides. Then a small amount of wood from the dead-sounding side will be removed during that break-in session.

Do not remove all of the excess width all at once. Many reeds will change their characteristics as the heart is slowly transformed during several break-in sessions. It is not unusual for a reed to begin with a dead sound on one side that disappears or switches to the other side. The goal in removing excess width is to remove the dead weight in such a manner so that the finished reed has a live sound on both sides.

Dealing With Extremely Weak Strength

Because of the exceptionally long and thin cut of a reed designed for a larger instrument, the initial blowing strength of a brand-new reed will be exceptionally weak even though the cane density is correct. The weakness is also created by a heart that is much too low on the profile. Furthermore, as warp removal is applied to the reed, it will become even weaker.

This means that all new reeds will have exceptionally weak strength for at least several break-in sessions. Then in later sessions, as the warp removal gradually lessens, clipping the tip will slowly move the heart upwardly into its correct position, at which time the strength will be dramatically increased.

The reed may be clipped and recut to micrometer specifications once or twice during each break-in session. And during the reed early break-in lifetime, its abstract will be thoroughly riddled with double minus signs and triple minus signs. To accelerate the strengthening process, the reed may be adjusted during the morning and evening of the same day.

Designing the Lower Blade

It is also advisable to begin designing ideal measurements for the lower blade. And in the interest of being thorough, these measurements should include the lower-blade quarter lines.

There is something satisfactory about the resonance and blowing ease of a thin lower blade. But as the hand made reed is clipped and the lower blade thickened as a result, this quality may begin to be lost. This is a good place to begin finalizing the first design of the lower-blade ideal measurements because a limit may have been reached.

138

For further improvement it is strongly suggested that experiments be made with a bite line that is 1 thousandth of an inch thinner than the first design.

How the Mouthpiece Facing Affects the Reed Strength

The mouthpiece facing affects the way in which the reed responds. There is a relationship between the length of the mouthpiece facing and the depth of the lower-blade cut that works like this.

A LONGER MOUTHPIECE FACING REQUIRES A MORE SUBSTANTIAL LOWER BLADE, AND A SHORTER MOUTHPIECE FACING REQUIRES A LESS SUBSTANTIAL LOWER BLADE.

This statement may be confirmed by observing the well-known twang test.

Place a 12-inch ruler on the desktop with one end hanging over the desk edge. While holding the ruler flat on the desktop with one hand, pull the overhanging end down with the other hand. Then suddenly let your fingers slip off the overhanging end.

The released energy will cause the ruler to vibrate with a twanging sound.

Observe that when a shorter length of the ruler is overhanging the desk edge, there is greater resistance; and a high-pitch twang will be produced. Or when a longer length is overhanging the edge, there is less resistance; and a low-pitch twang will be produced. These striking dissimilarities manifest even though there has been no change in the shape or density of the ruler.

When applying this principal to a reed design, it can be seen that the weaker strength of a thin lower blade may be compensated by shortening the mouthpiece facing. Or that the stiffer design of a thick lower blade may be compensated by lengthening the mouthpiece facing. Or to put it the other way around, a short mouthpiece facing might need a thinner lower blade (or lower density cane). And a long mouthpiece facing might need a thicker lower blade (or higher density cane).

Conclusions

Fully balanced hand made reeds take the most time to produce. But as stated before, the number of break-in sessions required to finish the reed is not the most important point. The most important point is that you keep working on the reed as long as there is positive development in its evolution.

Ideal lower-blade measurements may also be designed for tenor and baritone reeds. But these reeds are usually manufactured with sufficient wood to endure the fully balanced process without beginning with an oversized piece of cane.

And here is a reminder that an intended fully balanced reed may at any time be declared a quick-cut reed and placed into immediate use. The partially finished reed may still outplay any factory-cut reed in your present supply.

❖   ❖   ❖

APPENDIX

The Micrometer Assembly

The Dial Indicator

The dial indicator (which is also termed a thickness gauge in some catalogs) shown in Illustration 45 is a model designed for a 1-inch capacity. This model is

Illustration 45

A 1-INCH-CAPACITY DIAL INDICATOR

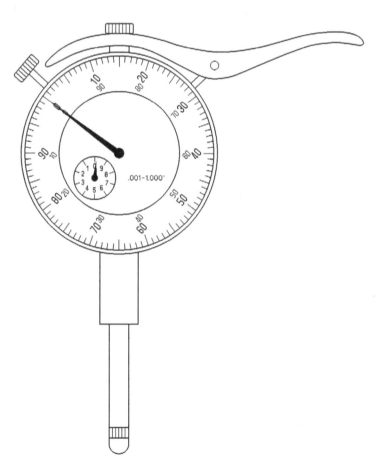

preferable to the smaller types because the longer plunger stem offers better visibility of the gridwork beneath the gauge, and the larger dial face is much easier to read. These gauges are found in auto-parts stores, hardware stores, and machine-tool supply houses. You will also need a magnetic stand that will be available from the same source as the dial indicator.

Features. If the model you select does not have these standard features, they should be available as accessories:

1. The dial face must be calibrated in thousandths of an inch;

2. The plunger tip must be of the half-round type that is nearly the same diameter as the plunger stem because this tip will slide easily over the reed surface; and

3. The backside of the dial face must have a mounting bracket for the magnetic-stand arm;

   (Another type of mounting is available that directly grasps the plunger housing, but this type is undesirable because it will block the view of the gridwork.)

The Magnetic Stand

This device is used to hold the dial indicator in a rigid, upright position. The device resembles a two-arm goal post with the two arms being connected by an adjustable swivel. The lower end of the vertical arm is imbedded in a heavy-duty magnet while the dial indicator is bolted to the cross arm by a second adjustable swivel.

The Temporary Gridwork

A temporary paper gridwork is available by photocopying Table 16. Be sure to bring a metric ruler to the copy center. When you have found a machine that produces a nearly exact 3-millimeter gridwork, make enough copies to serve as a long-time supply (if you must make a choice between sizes, a gridwork that is slightly smaller will be better than one that is slightly larger). This supply is necessary because the paper gridwork will become soiled, stretched, and abraded with use and will need periodic replacement.

The Permanent Gridwork

A paper gridwork is fine for producing accurate thickness curves, but a plastic gridwork will last for decades. As another benefit, the reed will slide over the smooth plastic with greater ease than on the sometimes-sticky paper.

A plastic gridwork[41] is constructed just like a mechanical drawing. You will need a drafting board, T square, metric ruler, good lighting, a large magnifying glass,[42] and paper tape.[43] But instead of using a pen or pencil, the gridwork lines will be scribed into the plastic by a large sewing needle that is held in a pin vise (handle). The scribes will then be filled in with two or three coats of black paint. And when the painted side is lightly sanded on the surface plate, thin, black lines will emerge. Then the gridwork will be screwed or glued to the stainless steel base plate.

One problem will arise in scribing the gridwork numbers. Since the numbers are so small and crowded, it might be wise to stagger them between the left and right sides of the gridwork. In any case, practice the number scribing on a piece of scrap plastic before numbering the permanent gridwork.[44]

---

[41] *A piece of sanded (to a frosted finish) clear plastic will contrast nicely between the light-colored wood and the black-painted lines. This contrasting will help to keep the reed straight on the gridwork. For a special touch, a piece of colored paper may be placed between the plastic gridwork and the stainless steel base plate.*

[42] *In order to keep both hands free, the large magnifying glass may be solidly taped to the top of a 1-pound can of coffee.*

[43] *The paper tape may be attached to the plastic just outside the actual gridwork area. Then accurate witness marks may be penciled on the tape to help align the ruler. And the ruler must also be securely taped to the plastic to keep it from slipping out of position.*

[44] *The plastic gridwork used in our shop was produced on a milling machine featuring metric cross slides. The large sewing needle was chucked in the headstock. And with the power turned off, the cross slides were used to produce long, even scratches on the plastic. The principal advantage is that a complete set of numbers were scratched on both sides of the gridwork; and the numbers came out looking exceptionally nice.*

This gridwork has seen decades of heavy-duty use, and during this time the micrometer stem has been accidentally slammed into the gridwork many times. The result of this damage, of course, has been a deep pit right at the 0/0 intersection. No matter, the pit has been carefully filled with cyanoacrylate glue (from the local hobby shop).

Illustration 46

THE MICROMETER-ASSEMBLY BASE PLATE

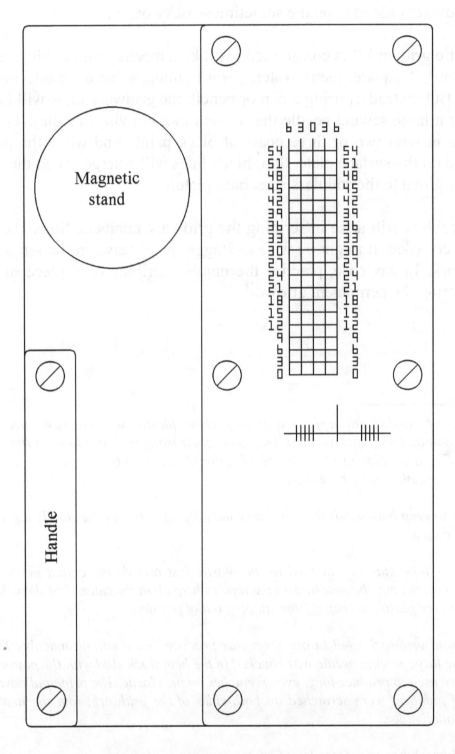

Not to scale; use your imagination in design; the components should be acquired before deciding the dimensions of the base plate; 3/16-inch-thick magnetic steel is rigid and will accept screws; pad the backside

Table 16

THREE-MILLIMETER-SQUARE GRIDWORKS

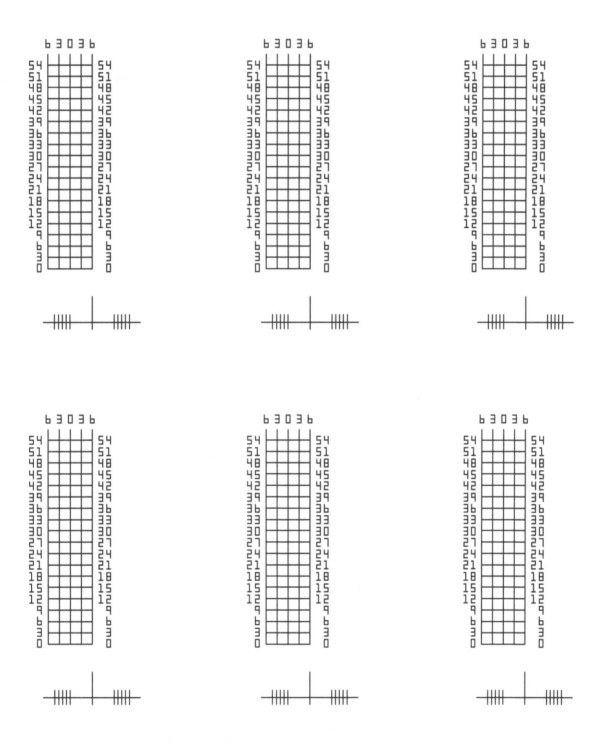

Illustration 47

THE CENTERLINE WITNESS MARK

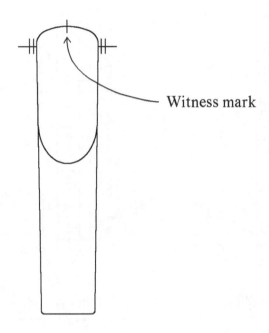

Witness mark

Center the reed between the guide lines; the pencil point must be sharp enough to make a thin line but not so sharp as to break off or cut into the reed

Designing a Tenor Sax Reed

The information in this section will enable the player to begin designing a personalized cut for increased performance potential. The method is noncomplex and requires no advanced mathematics. Be aware that the measurement numbers presented here are only examples. There are many variations available by changing the reed-tip, bite-line, and shoulder measurements, or by changing the bite-line and r-measurement formulas (the r-measurement formula is explained on page 153).

Although this method is shown for only tenor sax reeds, it may be used for all saxophone voices.

After this material has been thoroughly studied, the summary on page 154 may be used for quick reference.

Model Reeds

The best-playing reeds of your favorite brand and strength may be used as models in developing your own set of ideal measurements. In examining these factory-cut reeds with the micrometer, you will begin developing your own correct opinions about the upper-blade thickness curves.

Although it is possible to develop a set of ideal upper-blade measurements from only one or two excellent reeds, it is more probable that several excellent out-of-the-box reeds will be needed.

The Hooked Bite Line

To establish a resonant tone and correct support, the reed thickness must increase from the tip toward the lower areas. Although it might seem that a curve that progresses smoothly from the tip to the shoulder may be the best way of doing this, in practice it does not work. A smooth curve from the tip to the shoulder will produce a reed with a too-thin upper blade and a too-thick lower blade. Therefore, a modification is necessary; and that modification is to plot separate lengthwise curves for the upper and lower blades.

The division point between the upper and lower blades is the bite line. Although the straight-across bite line shown on page 7 is convenient for empirical evaluations, the straight-across line may produce a stiff and unresponsive reed when used with the micrometer method. An easy solution is to hook the edge lines downwardly from the 15-millimeter mark to the 18-millimeter mark (see the following page).

Applying the Model-Reed Measurements

Averaging the upper-blade cut. Draw separate upper-blade abstracts for each of the several excellent out-of-the-box reeds. On each of the abstracts, record the reed-tip measurements at the 6/0, 3/0, and 0/0 intersections of both sides of the reed. Then record the hooked-bite-line measurements at the 6/18 intersections, also from both sides of the reed.

(If any model reed has measurements that are significantly different from the other model reeds, that reed must not be included in the calculations.)

On a separate piece of paper, add all the individual intersection measurements (for example, seven abstracts will have 14 measurements for the 6/0 intersections). Then divide the sum by the number of measurements used.

Illustration 48

MICROMETER METHOD: THE HOOKED BITE LINE

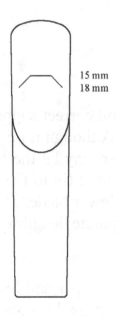

15 mm
18 mm

Plotting the Upper-Blade Curves

Draw a new abstract for the curves and fill in the measurements derived from the averaging process. The upper-blade curve may show a measurement that includes a half-thousandth of an inch, such as, 9+; but the bite-line measurement will always be a whole thousandth of an inch, such as, 29. If fractional measurements occur from the averaging process, round them upwardly toward the next-higher number.

Then fill in the blank measurements; and in a separate column on the right side, mark the increase for each downward 3-millimeter increment.

IN ORDER TO PRODUCE THE SMOOTHEST CURVE, EACH

LOWER 3-MILLIMETER INCREMENT MUST BE EQUAL TO OR

GREATER THAN THE PREVIOUS UPPER INCREMENT.

Table 17

PLOTTING THE UPPER-BLADE CURVES

```
             6                              6
        _____                      _____
    3  |  6                        3  |  6
                                              3+
    6  |                           6  |  9+
                                              4
    9  |                           9  | 13+
                                              4+
   12  |                          12  | 18
                                              5
   15  |                          15  | 23
                                              6
   18  |  29                      18  | 29
```

16a. Step 1   16b. Step 2

Enter the upper and   Fill in the smoothest
lower numbers   curve

The Bite-Line Formula

When a partial abstract is drawn for the bite line, thickness relationships among the bite-line measurements will be revealed. These relationships can then be expressed as a formula. Or better yet, the formula can be used to design the crosswise bite-line measurements.

The 0/2 formula shown on the next page is used as an example because it will maintain sufficient reed strength while providing protection against an upper-blade primary warp. Just as importantly, the moderate crosswise curve produced by the 0/2 formula provides excellent starting points for plotting the lengthwise lower-blade curves.

Also, the formula can be applied to bite lines of various thicknesses.

Illustration 49

THE CROSSWISE RELATIONSHIPS OF
THE BITE-LINE MEASUREMENTS

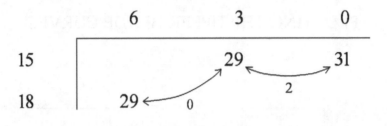

49a. The 0/2 formula

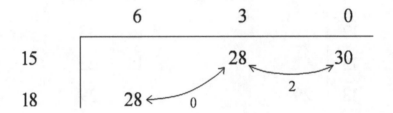

49b. Applying the 0/2 formula to a thinner bite line

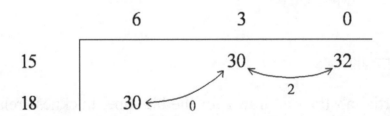

49c. Applying the 0/2 formula to a thicker bite line

The Transition Measurements

The transition measurements are the abstract measurements shown in parentheses. These are the devices that control the thickness and strength of the lower blade.

Table 18

TRANSITION MEASUREMENTS FOR A 0/2 BITE LINE AND RECOMMENDED LOWER-BLADE LENGTHS

Soprano

	4.5	0
3	x	x
6	x	x
9	x	x
12	x	x
15	x	x (9)
18	x (7)	x
21	x	x
24	x	x
27	x	x
30		x

Alto

	6	3	0
3	x	x	x
6	x	x	x
9	x	x	x
12	x	x	x
15	x	x (7)	x (8)
18	x (6)		x
21	x		x
24	x		x
27	x		x
30	x		x
33	x		x
36			x

Tenor

	6	3	0
3	x	x	x
6	x	x	x
9	x	x	x
12	x	x	x
15	x	x (7)	x (8)
18	x (6)		x
21	x		x
24	x		x
27	x		x
30	x		x
33	x		x
36			x

Baritone

	6	3	0
3	x	x	x
6	x	x	x
9	x	x	x
12	x	x	x
15	x	x (6)	x (7)
18	x (5)		x
21	x		x
24	x		x
27	x		x
30	x		x
33	x		x
36			x

Plotting the lower-blade quarter lines is optional

Baritone reeds may receive a 3-millimeter-longer lower blade if desired

A thinned stock will have a centerline that is 6 millimeters shorter than shown

The general lower-blade strength is controlled by the transition measurements, and your ideal set of transition measurements will be applied to all reeds of your usual boxed strength.

Adjustments for lower-blade strength. If your lower blades are consistently too weak, increase each transition measurement by 1 thousandth of an inch (i.e., a set of (6)/(7)/(8) transition measurements would become a set of (7)/(8)/(9) measurements).

Or if your lower blades are consistently too stiff, decrease each transition measurement by 1 thousandth of an inch (i.e., a set of (6)/(7)/(8) transition measurements would become a set of (5)/(6)/(7) measurements).

Plotting the Lower-Blade Curves

Table 19 shows the method for plotting lower-blade curves from the bite line to the 3-millimeter increment closest to the shoulder. As a matter of practicality, all lower-blade measurements will be expressed in whole thousandths of an inch. But the rule remains the same as that for the upper-blade curves. Each lower 3-millimeter increment must be equal to or greater than the previous upper increment. Additionally, jumps between increments are common. And all lower-increment jumps must be equal to or greater than the previous upper-increment jump (e.g., 6+1=7+2=9+2=11+3=14).

Table 19

PLOTTING THE LOWER-BLADE CURVES

	6			6			6			6	
18	27		18	28		18	29		18	29	
		(6)			(6)			(6)			(6)
21	33		21	34		21	35		21	35	
		7			7			7			8
24	40		24	41		24	42		24	43	
		9			9			9			10
27	49		27	50		27	51		27	53	
		11			11			12			12
30	60		30	61		30	63		30	65	
		14			15			15			15
33	74		33	76		33	78		33	80	

The Relationship Formula (r Formula)

The centerline measurement point is located 3 millimeters above the lower corners, not 3 millimeters below the corners as might be expected. This is because the upward location ensures better crosswise proportions of wood as expressed by the relationship formula or r formula.[45]

Generally, a factory-cut blade may have an abundance of centerline wood to ensure a well-centered pivot point. But this same abundance of wood also causes too much activity in the primary warp. So your ideal r-formula measurement will probably be thinner than the factory design.

Table 20 shows an example of $r = 8$ as a starting point for your own experiments. Once your ideal r-formula measurement has been discovered, it will be applied to all reeds of your usual boxed strength no matter how thick or thin the lower-corner measurements of a particular reed may be.

Table 20

THE RELATIONSHIP BETWEEN THE LOWER CORNERS
AND THE CENTERLINE MEASUREMENT POINT

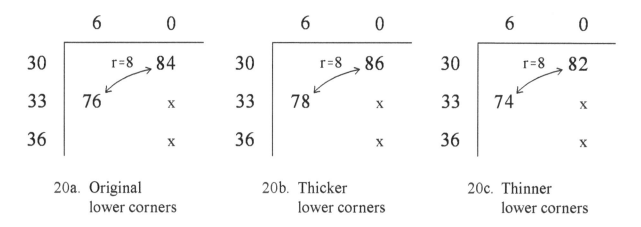

20a. Original   20b. Thicker   20c. Thinner
      lower corners   lower corners   lower corners

The centerline measurement point is located 3 millimeters above the lower corners; the value of r must be found by experiment; $r = 8$ is only a suggestion that might be suitable for alto or tenor reeds; a soprano reed might be $r = 9$; or a baritone reed might be $r = 7$

---

[45] *The thickness measurements for the 33/0 and 36/ intersections (shown as Xs in the Table 20 examples) may be determined by plotting a logical, continued curve toward the shoulder edge.*

Table 21

SUMMARY: DESIGINING A TENOR SAX REED

	6	3	0
3	6	6+	6+
6			
9			
12			
15		29	31
		2	
18	29	0	

21a. The average reed-tip and hooked-bite-line edge measurements from several excellent out-of-the-box-reeds are entered; the bite-line formula is applied

	6	3	0
3	6	6+	6+
	3+	4+	5
6	9+	11	11+
	4	5	6
9	13+	16	17+
	4+	6	6+
12	18	22	24
	5	7	7
15	23	29	31
	6		
18	29		

21b. The smoothest upper-blade curves are entered

	6	3	0
15		29	31
		(7)	(8)
18	29		
	(6)		
21			
24			
27			
30		r = 8	84
33	76		
36			

21c. The transition measurements, lower-corner measurements for the individual reed, and r-formula are entered

	6	3	0
15		29	31
		(7)	(8)
18	29		39
	(6)		9
21	35		48
	7		10
24	42		58
	9		12
27	51		70
	11		14
30	62		84
	14		17
33	76		101
			21
36			122

21d. The smoothest lower-blade curves are entered

A Special Consideration for Soprano Sax Reeds

A soprano sax reed is too narrow for full crosswise measurement on the 3-millimeter gridwork. But the centerline witness mark may be placed at the estimated 4.5-millimeter lines to produce three lengthwise curves instead of the usual five.

Also, the bite-line-formula method detailed on pages 149 and 150 is not possible when there are only three lengthwise measurement lines. Instead, a soprano sax reed will use an r-formula measurement to design an ideal bite line. The measurements will be made at the 4.5/18 and 0/15 intersections, and the value of r might be 2 or 3 thousandths of an inch.

Illustration 50

MEASURING A SOPRANO SAX REED

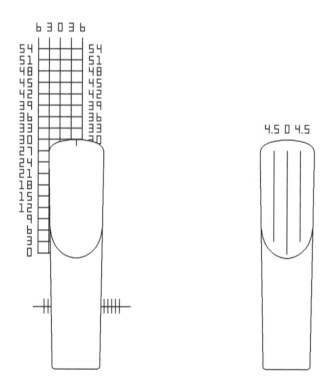

The centerline witness mark is positioned
at the estimated 4.5-millimeter mark

❖　　　❖　　　❖

Encino, California
July 1995

Fellow Saxophonists:

The findings in this book are the result of over thirty years' experience preparing reeds for performance in intense musical environments; such as, Stan Kenton, Supersax, Louis Bellson, Bill Holman, Bob Florence, Hollywood studios, and many other organizations whose names are not listed here. So be assured that the proving grounds for these reeds have been rigorous and diverse.

At first reading, the large amount of information and interrelated concepts may seem bewildering. But continued study will reveal that for the reeds selected to break in, there are really only two major problems with which to contend. The first problem concerns reeds with excess warping tendencies, and the second problem concerns reeds in which the cane quality is somehow incorrect. And if these two problems could be avoided (which, unfortunately, they cannot), then intelligent application of the adjustment techniques should ensure the positive evolution of the reeds even though the techniques may not be applied with complete perfection.

Also, since so many of these adjustments are very easy to perform, it seems that some version of a quick-cut reed should be possible for nearly everyone.

Ray Reed

idig

SYNOPSIS ON THE SCIENCE OF ADJUSTING SAXOPHONE REEDS

Ray Reed

I. Introduction

Dead Weight: A Major Problem

Dead weight is one of the three major problems in saxophone reeds (the other two are bad sections of cane and excess warping tendencies). And because of inconsistencies and incapabilities in automatic-reed-manufacturing technologies, nearly all machine-cut reeds emerge from the processes with an abundance of unneeded wood.

Unneeded wood and the water it contains are parasitic because energy is stolen from the player's breath just to move this useless mass around for a free ride during reed vibration. Excess bending resistance is also created by unneeded mass. But that is not all. The extra mass is always located in the wrong places (there are no right places), and the inertia rates for the different reed areas will be thrown out of balance with one another.

The result of these simultaneous complications is that the reed will be incapable of bouncing lightly at its open-most and closed positions. Instead, it will crash and crash against these positions with every wave of the vibration cycle; and the tone quality will therefore become distorted.

As a metaphor, consider the bouncing of a basketball. It takes just a flick of energy from the wrist and arm to keep the ball bouncing back up into your hand; and each time the ball strikes the concrete, it makes a pleasant, percussive sound.

SYNOPSIS ON THE SCIENCE OF ADJUSTING SAXOPHONE REEDS

Next, imagine that same basketball filled partway with water. Now the ball must be slammed and slammed to keep it bouncing back into your hand; and each time the ball strikes the concrete, it makes a thudding, splattering sound.

The vibration performance of an overweight, water-laden saxophone reed is much like the bouncing performance of an overweight, water-laden basketball. It is just happening on a different scale.

Finally, that extra material is literally killing the sound of the saxophone in a damping action. As long as excess material is present in the reed, it does not matter how much air pressure is forced into the instrument. Full resonance will never be achieved until the unwanted mass is removed.

Solutions and Secondary Problems

A great deal of weight will be removed from the backside of the reed during warp removal. Nearly complete warp removal might involve several or more break-in sessions, and a cumulative massive amount of wood will be eliminated during these sessions. This usually means that the reed heart will emerge as being too thin for itself while also losing its correct relationship with the outer areas of the blade (the lengthwise edges and reed tip).

The solution to this effect is also cumulative. After the backside warp has been recut during each break-in session, the reed tip may be clipped to rethicken the heart. And here is where the secondary problems arise. After the tip has been clipped, the outer areas may become too thick and heavy while the length of the cut (from the reed tip edge to the shoulder edge) may eventually become too short.

There is only one satisfactory way to maintain correct thickness of the reed blade during these operations. That is to micrometer the entire surface of the blade and to keep cutting down the emerging thick areas to match a set of ideal measurements that have proved to be best. (This assumes that the cane selected is the correct density, i.e., not too tough or not too pulpy. Otherwise, the ideal lengthwise micrometer curves may require modifications.)

Observe what is happening here. Correcting a warp removes material from the backside of the reed heart. And to return this area to its correct thickness, the front side of the heart is then allowed to increase its mass. Concurrently, the lengthwise thickness curves are maintained at precise micrometer specifications.

This process will be repeated, break-in session after break-in session, until the warping has nearly stabilized or until the player otherwise determines that the reed is ready for performance.

II. A Fully Balanced Reed: An Ideal Comparator

It is well-known that there is nothing to be done that will enhance the good qualities of a saxophone reed. We cannot zap it with "good" plasma, nor can we sprinkle it with fairy dust. All the goodness that the finished reed will possess is already present within its fibers. The beneficial things that can be done, however, are to eliminate surplus material and to reshape the remaining mass in order to minimize the detrimental qualities of the reed.

In applying this cutting, it is the goal of the saxophonist to help the reed to play better. But that is a naive statement. Play better than what? To just exactly what is it that any resulting improvements or detriments must be compared? The time has come to think this matter through more thoroughly.

Interdependent Forces

When a reed is being played, that reed will be exhibiting several specific physical forces. These forces will all be emanating from the same piece of cane and will be all manifesting at the same time. When the names of these forces are known (explained on page 163), it is possible to make a list of them, thus individualizing them. But in practice it is not so simple. That is, if it is decided to adjust one of these forces, often the worst one, then all of the several forces will be automatically changed at the same time, some to a greater degree or some to a lesser degree according to the nature of that particular piece of cane. Therefore, they are not independent forces. Rather, they are *Interdependent Forces*, which means that it is impossible to adjust only one force at a time.

The Difference Between a Good Reed and a Bad Reed

If a particular project reed exists in a state or evolves to a state wherein the interdependent forces are cooperating and complementing one another, then this will be a good playing reed or possibly a great playing reed. And the opposite is also true.

If a particular project reed exists in a state or evolves to a state wherein the interdependent forces are fighting and antagonizing one another, then this will be a bad playing reed.

The Near Myth of the Perfect Reed

A reed going through the break-in process is a reed in evolution. Although there may be occasional side issues with which to deal, the following sequence of events is the projected course of the evolution.

* A brand-new reed will have major imbalances within the interdependent forces.

* During the first break-in sessions, the major imbalances will become only moderate imbalances.

* As the break-in sessions continue, the moderate imbalances will become only minor imbalances.

* With even more break-in sessions, the minor imbalances will become only micro-imbalances.

A reed that has evolved to such an advanced state so that only micro-imbalances remain shall be termed a *Fully Balanced Reed*. The question arises, however, that if even more break-in sessions are spent, should not the micro-imbalances also be removed; and the only thing left is an absolutely perfect reed with no imbalances at all? The answer is yes. But these reeds are not practical to use as comparators for the following reasons.

As soon as the perfect reed is placed into serious play, vibration stresses are going to begin ripping its fibers apart. And within only a few minutes playing time, the micro-imbalances will return because of the physical destruction incurred. Or if the perfect reed is not played at all, the period of dryness it will be experiencing will regenerate the warping tendencies; and this will also cause micro-imbalances to return.

Conclusions

When making and adjusting saxophone reeds, it is necessary to have an identifiable goal or scale of measure to use for comparison. Just exclaiming that a reed plays better or worse after an adjustment or daydreaming of a perfect reed are insufficient. Fully balanced reeds are the best comparators and can be produced by using the correct tools and procedures.

On a scale of 1 to 100, unadjusted factory-cut reeds most often score below 50. Fully balanced reeds consistently score from 80 to 100.

III. Descriptions of Terms and Physical Forces

These terms are used in the formulas on page 165.

General

Fully balanced reed:	A reed that has evolved through the adjustment process so that only micro-imbalances remain.
Warp relieved:	Refers to recutting the reed backside after warping has occurred. There are five types of backside warps, three concave types and two convex types. Most reeds have more than one type at the same time, and they are often maximized at different places along the lengthwise and crosswise axes.
Microbalanced:	Using a micrometer to reproduce ideal lengthwise thickness curves derived from other successful reeds. Upper blades can be adjusted to tolerances of less than one-half thousandth of an inch in thickness. Lower-blade measurements are less stringent.
Proportioned:	Refers to the lengthwise proportions of wood between the upper blade and lower blade.
Resonance:	The reed and instrument air column work together to produce the sound of the saxophone. The principal function of the reed vibration is to amplify the natural vibrations of the air column into full audibility. Once amplified, the air column will cause the reed to vibrate at the same frequency as the air column itself. The purpose of reed adjustment is to make the reed responsive to resonance and vibration in cooperation with the air column and oral cavity.

Tonal range: Low Bb to high F.

Dynamic range: Perhaps pp to fff.

Note: Here is another way in which interdependence works. Observe that it is impossible to play any tone on the saxophone without establishing a dynamic level for that tone, and it is also impossible to establish a dynamic level without playing a tone through which that dynamic level is expressed. One force cannot exist without the other, and the other force cannot exist without the one.

Aspects of Interdependence

These aspects may be divided into principal forces and secondary forces as shown in the equation on page 165.

Tone: This is the only force that is judged solely by artistic interpretation. The tone is either pleasing, or it is not; or it is some state inbetween. There is no rule of physics to apply.

Strength: The strength (bending resistance) of the reed should be about equal to the embouchure strength while the embouchure is held in a comfortable and efficient manner. This is an aspect of balancing.

Intonation: Intonation is the most rigid criterion. It may be better to compromise some other quality of the reed performance rather than play out of tune.

Bite line: Refers to the amount inserted into the mouth. Short cuts and thick lower blades will shorten the bite. Warps usually lengthen the bite.

The illusion of
the reed tip: An aspect of proportioning wherein a thick lower blade may make the reed tip feel too thin when it actually is not. Or a thin lower blade may make the reed tip feel too thick when it also is not.

High-note, low-
note balancing: Another aspect of proportioning concerning the blowing of low Bb and high F without excess manipulation of the embouchure. The relative intonation of low Bb and high F is also controlled by proportioning.

IV. Explanation of Reed's Theory

Reed's Theory is a simplified version of the criteria of a fully balanced reed, and it is stated here in both paragraph form and equation form. In the equation form the criteria on the left side of the equal sign is equal to the fully balanced reed on the right side, and the fully balanced reed on the right side of the equal sign is equal to the criteria on the left side. There are no superfluous items in the criteria, and no significant aspects have been omitted. The equation may be disassembled and reassembled with no loss of integrity.

V. Reed's Theory

A FULLY BALANCED REED IS ONE THAT HAS BEEN WARP RELIEVED, MICROBALANCED, AND PROPORTIONED IN SUCH A MANNER SO THAT THE RESONANCE IS FULLY ESTABLISHED THROUGHOUT THE TONAL AND DYNAMIC RANGES AND SO THAT THE ASPECTS OF INTERDEPENDENCE ALIGN AND BALANCE WITH ONE ANOTHER.

Warp relieved
Microbalanced
Proportioned

Resonance

    Tonal range
    Dynamic range

Aspects of interdependence

Principal forces

Tone	Equal	Fully
Strength	$=$	Balanced
Intonation	$\leftrightarrow$	Reed

Secondary forces

    Bite line

    The illusion of
    the reed tip

    High-note, low-note
    balancing

VI. Closing

The shape and mass of a saxophone reed determine its responsiveness to resonance and vibration, and the player can be in great control of these aspects. With the correct knowledge and equipment, each stroke of the cutting tools will bring that reed one step closer to being the best reed that it can be.

Using the micrometer method and a good set of ideal measurements is the fastest and most reliable method of reed adjustment. If fact, the entire front surface of the blade can be measured and recut before any break-in sessions are spent at all; and a better impression of the finished product will be revealed at the very beginning.

Empirical adjustments without a micrometer can also show substantial gains in performance just by paying attention to the equation criteria as a reed is being adjusted. Even though a fully balanced reed may never be produced using the empirical method, use your best reed as a comparator and keep trying to make a better one.

When using either the empirical method or micrometer method, problems in the cane quality and/or excess warping tendencies may be discovered. If a particular reed is showing pronounced detriments in these areas, toss it out and go to work on a hopefully more profitable piece of cane.

❖   ❖   ❖

THE SEARCH

My life as a woodwind player began as a pre-teenager playing clarinet with school bands in the suburbs of Los Angeles during the early 1950s. My clarinet was a Selmer Signet with a Selmer HS** mouthpiece and Rico No. 2 1/2 reeds. I had a lot of facility in my fingers and a good ear for music. My tone quality was more like a Dixielander than a classical player. Being self-taught, I wasn't too concerned about my tone at the time. But that was soon to change. The change was a big one, too. It happened when I found that my talent and heart's desire was to be an alto saxophone player.

There was an excellent Tuesday-night dance band at Reseda High School under the direction of Leonard Gagliardi; and approaching my senior year at that school, I wanted to be in that band more than anything else in the world. So I got myself together and rented a Buescher alto sax that turned out to be not so good. That was followed by a Martin Streamline alto with a Selmer Soloist E mouthpiece and Rico No. 2 1/2 reeds, and then I was in business for real.

Playing alto in the dance band was a most wonderful experience. I dreamed about it day and night. And I was absolutely falling in love with jazz and swing music. But no matter how soaring my emotions were becoming, things were not going so well with my performance. My bottom lip hurt like crazy; the high notes would sometimes get so sharp that I couldn't stand it; and it seemed that the longer I played, the worse things became.

About the same time I began studying woodwinds at the Reseda House of Music with John Setar, who was playing with Jerry Gray, Freddy Martin, and others of the genre. And when John was too busy to give lessons, I would sometimes go in for a session with Clint Neagley of the Benny Goodman band, who also taught at that store.

I began telling John about the physical problems I was experiencing, and I was glad that I did. The first thing that he suggested was to get rid of the Selmer mouthpiece with its long facing and try something else. The first try was a Beechler hard-rubber experimental model, and that was followed by a Brilhart Ebolin 4 (black plastic with a white patch on the beak). I settled in with the Brilhart and my blowing problems became less severe. But nonetheless, I was still hurting and playing sharp on the high notes.

Next, John showed me how to sand a bit off the backside of the reed and to cut the upper heart into more of a Christmas tree shape. Then came the purchase of a reed clipper. This was a period of total revelation to me. I had never known that experimenting with equipment could show such dramatic improvements in my performance.

After leaving high school I joined the musicians' union and began getting a bit of work with no-name bands playing social engagements. I couldn't make enough money to meet expenses this way, though, so I also had a variety of odd jobs like most young people did. One of these jobs was to be a flunky at a nearby aerospace machine shop called Radiatronics. This turned out to be a fortunate situation because there I learned something about lathes, milling machines, micrometers, and such; and this knowledge proved to be very useful in the later conception of my reed-measuring tool.

At the same time, I began playing with college bands just for the enjoyment and to further develop my musical skills. I was first-chair saxophone at nearby Pierce College under the direction of Ted Dechter, Valley Community College under the direction of Bob McDonald, Valley State College (later known as California State University Northridge) under the direction of Bob Delwarte, and also first-chair second clarinet in the Valley State College concert band under the direction of Clarence Wiggins. During this time I was practicing my brains out on clarinet, saxophone, and flute. I was also becoming compelled by jazz playing. Scales, chords, and tunes were always running through my mind. Listening to jazz records was another big trip.

My stand mate in the concert band was an older gentleman from Austria named Franz Zeidler who played a Mueller system clarinet with a neck strap. I tried a couple of his mouthpieces and found them to be too "dead" for me. Then he invited me to his apartment one evening to try out some reeds. What an experience. Now I know how he managed to sound so good on that lame clarinet and mouthpiece. The reeds had such an exceptionally live, resonant tone and were so free and controllable that the other detriments to his playing seemed insignificant. His method, he explained, was to begin with the best piece of cane he could find, either cut from a tube or from a box of Vandorens, and carefully sand and massage the reed into shape on a piece of flat glass while treating the reed with hydrogen peroxide. I never did get to study old-school reed making seriously with Franz because I left college to play on a road band. And when I came back, Franz had passed away. Nonetheless, those reeds were permanently engraved in my mind. I knew if I were to continue my career and to compete with established players, I needed to have reeds that played like that. I also knew that I would have to teach myself how to make them.

Playing with the college bands was also a big help in becoming an established player myself. At a rehearsal at Valley Community College one summer afternoon, Shorty Rogers came by to have some of his new charts played. He was going to record these charts for a music-publishing company and asked our band to them proofread them. Surprisingly, Shorty hired some of us to do the recording session; and I was overwhelmed that I was included in those who were selected.

Playing with Shorty softened the blow for the next surprise. At a Valley State College rehearsal one evening, Jim Amlotte, road manager of the Stan Kenton Orchestra, came by to listen to the band. Stan was putting together a new orchestra for a road trip in 1965 and was looking for some young people who played with a lot of fire. I suspect that Bob Delwarte knew this, and the chart he called to play was Gerald Wilson's "Nancy Jo" to show me off. This up-tempo blues tune has a saxophone soli running up and down be bop chord changes, and I knew it by heart. A few of us were invited to audition for a chair, and I was once again overwhelmed that I was selected. Goodbye, college!

Playing with Stan's band was an extremely difficult period for me. I had to be an immaculate lead player on quiet, waterfall-like sax solis on the dance charts and follow that up with maximum volume on the concert charts while trying to keep up with ten overpowering brass players. I also had to be a hot and cool jazz player in the tradition of predecessors like Bud Shank, Art Pepper, and Lee Konitz. So the problem to me was trying to develop an all-around playing style that would encompass these broad diversifications. The best part about the situation was that I didn't have to play clarinet.

So, what was the answer? It took twenty more years to find out.

At the beginning of this stint with Stan, I was playing on a Selmer alto with my Brilhart mouthpiece and Rico No. 2 1/2 reeds and performing successfully on this setup too. But I was still getting back on the bus with a sore lip (I wasn't alone on that issue either—the trumpet players would often be snapping out over their chops). When we hit Chicago one day, my friends in the sax section insisted that we go see Frank Wells to get some mouthpieces cut. I didn't know who Frank was at the time. But when we went into his basement shop, I handed him my Brilhart and got another of the biggest lessons of my life. He cut the bed flat, measured the chamber with a home made protractor, recut the facing, and filed down the sides of the beak, all the while asking me to keep testing the mouthpiece so he could listen to it. When finished, this mouthpiece played better than I would have believed. Not only did this refresh my memory that equipment could be modified for great improvements in performance but also reinforced my opinion that I must learn how to do these things for myself. The next thing I did was to buy a mouthpiece refacing kit from the Eric Brand company for future use.

The reborn Brilhart lasted for many months, but then it developed a warp from all the temperature changes while on the road. I moved on to a hard-rubber Meyer 5M mouthpiece and began getting a better jazz sound as a bonus. But I was becoming less concerned about mouthpiece problems and more concerned about reed problems.

In a break at home after that tour, I bought a miniature milling machine called a Unimat that featured metric cross slides. This machine was used to make the 3-millimeter-square gridwork for use with a micrometer in measuring reed-blade thicknesses. The construction was a complete success, but I really didn't know how to use the new reed-measuring tool. During this break I also began studying flute and piccolo with renowned Ben Kanter. The best things I learned from Ben were about discipline and self-criticism as an all-around musician, not just as a flutist.

During the next tour with Stan, he gave me a raise in salary. Now I could afford to have my own hotel rooms and buy lots more reeds. In my suitcase I carried the glass surface plate from the Eric Brand mouthpiece kit and the home made reed micrometer. I would spend great amounts of time alone in my room working on my supply of reeds while practicing quietly to avoid disturbing other hotel guests. Most of this time I was concerned with getting a better air seal on the backsides of the reeds and balancing their edges. But it was tedious work, and I kept falling behind schedule.

I started searching music stores on the road, trying to find books or publications on reed adjustments. The reed books that I found were limited in scope, sometimes contradictory, and contained more wishful thinking than scientific fact. The general scientific-type books that I found were way over my head, full of mathematic equations and wave-length analyses that seemed to be of little use in reed making.

During my last two tours with Stan, I suppose I just gave up because of the drudgery and limited success that I was having with reeds and developed a new tactic. I moved down a half-strength to Rico No. 2 reeds. I would work on nearly a whole box at a time in my room, flattening the backsides and clipping the tips. The micrometer was abandoned in favor of eyeballing and test playing the reeds.

At the concerts I kept a cigar box full of these "quick-cut" reeds under my stand and would toss my present reed out when it became too weak or began to play flat. During this time I taught myself to do an upper-blade-angle reset on the bandstand, often intentionally cracking the blade into a mild V shape to maintain strength and pitch for a few more minutes. Whether I would take a quick time-out to crack a reed or exchange it for a new one, I got to be really fast at reed changes. A wetted reed and an eight-bar rest were all I needed. Cork grease on the ligature screws helped a lot too.

After quitting Stan in 1968, I settled down again in suburban Los Angeles. There were plenty of opportunities to play. I had a full schedule of rehearsals, casuals, club dates, and even some studio work. But most importantly, I had time to practice my doubles and try to figure out what to do with the reed micrometer. Some of the bands I played with in those days were Bill Holman, Don Menza, Dee Barton, Gerald Wilson, and Frank Zappa. I also improved my collection of instruments. I wound up with four Selmer saxes, a Buffet clarinet, a Powell flute, and a Muramatsu alto flute. With each change in equipment, my playing level would go up and up.

But now back to reed cutting. The biggest problem I faced was the warping of reed backsides. Slowly, I began to recognize that the cut on a reed should not be finalized until the warp had been completely removed. This was contrary to my indoctrination. I guess I had placed too much faith in reed manufacturers' literature that their reeds play best. These claims, I now believed, were pure advertising mumbo jumbo. Nevertheless, the convex bulging of warmed-up reeds was a continuous problem; and my playing abilities were not at their best because of it.

I developed a way to look at the reed/mouthpiece combination in the desk lamp to see how far the reed had warped since its last cutting, and the theory of static and dynamic shapes became a reality. If a rested reed shows a concavity in the backside during its static shape, it will result in a flatter shape when it reaches its dynamic shape. What could be simpler? But I couldn't figure out why. Then a stroke of luck came my way. I was reading a model-airplane magazine one day. In the readers'-write column, one modeler asked why the solid-wood rudder on his airplane kept warping and throwing the plane out of control. The editor's answer was that the cross section centerline and the center of mass were in different places; and when the weather changed, the rudder would try to equalize itself. The statement was supplemented by a cross section drawing of a rudder, flat on one side and curved on the other, which strongly resembled the cross section of a saxophone reed. "This is something that most engineers know" [sic]. You better believe that this knowledge hit me hard. The more I thought about it, the more I became convinced that it was true. And saxophone reeds must be even more vulnerable to this effect because of the violent twisting and water soaking they receive. (If I still had this magazine, I would have used a footnote in my book to cite the source. But I didn't know at the time that I would someday write a book on the subject, and the magazine became lost and its title forgotten.)

Next came a more thorough investigation of warps. The tangent warp was the next significant discovery, which was shocking to me. All these years I had been staring at tangent warps without recognizing them because I was too preoccupied with convex warps. But experiments in carefully removing convex warps confirmed the reality of the tangent warps lurking beneath them, even though these experiments caused the willing destruction of many good reeds in the process.

While thinking these things through more thoroughly, I began considering opposing forces. It was now clear to me that the convex warp and the concave warp were opposite expressions of the same thing and that these forces were proportional to each other. These considerations with opposing forces gave me the first glimmerings of what was to become the theory of interdependence. As a side issue, I was driving myself nuts with the terms "convex" and "concave." This mental tongue twister involving two words beginning with "c" was too much for me to handle, so I began calling the convex warp the "primary warp" and have had more peace of mind ever since.

Did the tangent warp have an opposing force? This one took a long time to prove because reeds displaying this opposite were rare, coming to me as though by accident. This opposite is termed an arched stock. And I could not be sure of my findings with only a couple of examples. I needed several or a dozen (I can't remember how many). But nonetheless, an arched stock proved to be a reality; and the theory of interdependence became more solidified.

The pocket warp was discovered by a fortunate twitch of my thumb. It happened while checking a reed on the mouthpiece by using the desk lamp. I inadvertently squeezed the pocket area and observed the reed springing away from the mouthpiece. Further examination revealed my first pocket warp. This one was easy to figure out. All I had to do was sand pocket warps into a stack of reeds to see what happened. In nearly every case the results were the same. This was a weakening of the tone quality (some of these reeds, though, still played well even with their new pocket warps). This was an important discovery to me because in past years I may have tossed out many reeds, blaming bad cane for their poor performance when all the time it may have been pocket warps causing their problems. Did the pocket warp have an opposite? It seems that it does not. So it appeared that the theory of interdependence was not going to be a simple answer. Rather, it was going to be complex.

The tip-edge profiler was an important find, too. One day I became curious about the accuracy of the reed micrometer in measuring tip edges. There was already a .005" feeler gauge lying next to the micrometer assembly, so I put the gauge on the surface plate and butted a reed tip edge against it to explore the junction with my fingernail. Next, I pulled out a .004" gauge and taped down both gauges so they wouldn't slide around. It didn't take much experimenting to find that I preferred the .004" gauge and that a piece of flattened rush would cut the reed without harming the metal gauge. I taped the .004" feeler gauge to a piece of scrap plastic and have been using that tool and measurement for reeds on all my instruments ever since. I shared the knowledge of this technique with some other players, and those who tried it returned great compliments about their successes.

Toward the end of the 1970s, work in the Los Angeles area was slowing down to a more comfortable pace. This gave me more free time for practicing, composing, instrument repairs, or just resting my overworked chops.

To keep things interesting, though, in 1978 I received the first-tenor chair with Med Flory's Supersax. Playing with this band was intriguing because I had found a group wherein the music we played matched (or sometimes exceeded) my own level of playing. This was a great fulfillment to me. The down side was that I had to set my other studies aside in order to become a better tenor player than ever before.

I used a Selmer Mark VI tenor with a brass mouthpiece designed and hand cut by Don Menza. This mouthpiece has a short bite and a really ragged facing. It is lacking in the warm-tone department. But when played with Rico No. 2 Plasticover reeds (quick-cut modifications), I found the fast response that I needed. And believe me, you don't appreciate what fast response really means until you play blazing runs all over the horn, page after page, tune after tune as we did with that band. After settling in with this equipment, a few months of daily practice helped to learn the Supersax library. My tenor playing had been kicked up a few notches; and to my delight, some of this newfound expertise was overflowing into my performance on my other instruments.

The micrometer had not been idle during all this time. But it would be another ten years before the theory of interdependence would be more fully understood.

My initial thoughts about the micrometer were based upon the principle that reed manufacturers knew a great deal more than I about the mechanics and shaping of saxophone reeds; and if I could study the shaping of enough excellent, out-of-the-box factory-cut reeds (mostly concentrating on alto sax reeds), some mystery might be solved or some secret might be revealed. Furthermore, I was exceptionally timid about cutting reeds to shape, believing that if I strayed too far from the manufacturers' specifications, a performance-ready reed might somehow be destroyed. Then I might be at a loss for a good reed at one of my next concerts.

These attitudes, I later found, were not the best. First, a reed plays the way it does because of what it is in its present state. It does not matter if the factory cut the reed or if I did it myself or someone else cut it. Secondly, removing only small amounts of wood turned out to be exactly the opposite of what was really needed to investigate the mechanics of reed performance. Correct analyses require that massive amounts of wood be removed for proper interpretations of the results. This meant, unfortunately, that I had to maintain two supplies of reeds: those that were for professional use and those that were for experimental use. As you might see, this led to many long hours of daily reed cutting.

Using factory-cut reeds as models turned out to be quite confusing. Within a box of ten or twenty-five reeds, there would be many variations in thickness measurements. And the variations would continue from box to box. Then I came upon the bright idea that the intersection measurements from a large supply of reeds might be averaged, and the resulting averages might be what I was searching for. This turned out to be a very good idea, indeed. While recording these averaged measurements on a piece of paper, my first micrometer abstract was created, and I began calling the measurements "ideal measurements." This was the gateway that led to blueprinting each of my reeds to match a specific numeric shape.

While measuring these many boxes of reeds, I did discover that the upper part of their blades showed more consistency in shaping than the lower part of their blades. This was the clue that I had been hoping to find, and I began giving my full attention to the upper-blade shaping. The only obstacle was in defining exactly where the division line between the two areas should be. That was easy. Just by eyeballing the reed and gridwork, it was apparent that the 15-millimeter mark was the best place. (This later evolved into the hooked bite line that helped eliminate some unneeded stiffness. The idea was to make the bite line resemble the outline of the upper heart. I never did figure out if this curve was supposed to be elliptical or parabolic. But it didn't matter to me. The hooked bite line worked, and that is really all that I needed to know.) The lower blades of these reeds were cut on an individual basis. Although the bite-line measurements were uniformly fixed among all my reeds, the shoulder measurements and lower-blade curves were adjusted for each particular reed.

But now new problems began getting my attention. Those problems concerned upper-blade primary warps.

I tried a few experiments in thinning upper hearts from both the front sides and backsides to reduce the warp severity and found that the thinning worked. But when using my favorite No. 2 1/2 reeds, their strengths kept declining, and their lifetimes were too short for my satisfaction. On my next trip to the music store, I picked up a box of No. 3 reeds to see if increasing the density would help maintain stiffness in a thinned upper heart. The answer was yes. But it was not enough. So I quickly moved up another half-strength to No. 3 1/2 reeds and found much better results. As a bonus, I began getting a fuller tone quality without increasing my physical effort.

Although the results were better, there was still something missing. And I suppose my psychology had something to do with my next phase. It would have been easy to accept this reed design for the rest of my playing life and devote most of my time to hard practice sessions. But my spirit continued to soar beyond my control. I needed to play even better, and that was that. So it was decided to engage in more reed experiments just to see if anything was left to be discovered.

During a period of deep contemplation, I began considering the thickness of the bite line. In this state of mind, it became clear that a thinner bite line combined with even lengthwise curves would reduce the mass of both the upper and lower blades at the same time and that faster response and greater playing ease might be the result. This idea proved to be correct. It took some fiddling around with the numbers on my abstracts to get things right, and an old empirical lesson returned to my mind. That lesson was that you could remove a slice of wood from the centerline of the reed right at the bite line to reduce the strength and quicken the response. If the length of the bite changed, elongating the length of the cut area toward its top or bottom end would restore the bite to its correct position. Even though I had no words at the time to describe these impressions, this was the beginning of the theories of proportioning.

The next discovery, as I remember, involved thinning the stocks and improvising the cutting jig just to see if the primary warp could be further minimized by moving the stock center of mass closer to its cross section centerline. These experiments were prompted by the success gained in thinning the upper hearts. Once again, these thoughts proved to be correct. But a couple of surprises also happened. The first surprise was that there was more ringing in my sound from the removal of unneeded damping material. The second occurred when I filed down the ragged upper edge of a new rainbow-shaped shoulder to make it look better. The sound rung even more while the blowing ease and intonation of the low register also made noticeable improvements.

I kept trying different configurations, hoping to find even better performance. But instead, I was hit by a major setback.

With all the warp removal, tip clipping, lengthwise-curve cutting, and stock thinning, my sound became too small for me to tolerate. (I didn't know about the resonance-reversal point at that time, but it was later discovered that this was one of the problems. There was another significant problem occurring in these now-tiny, overcut reeds, but I never did understand what it was.) A search for a better ligature than my Selmer proved to be unsuccessful. Next, the density was increased to No. 4 and No. 5 reeds, but my adjustment techniques were not enough to conquer this tough and unyielding cane.

Now, with nothing but my suspicions to guide me, it was determined that the best course of action would be to try making my own reeds by beginning with oversized pieces of cane. I picked up a box of No. 3 1/2 tenor reeds and began hacking away at them, hoping somehow to come up with a good alto reed. The work was slow and tedious, and I made a lot of beginner's mistakes. But after some experience and confidence had been gained, the reeds began to respond correctly; and my speed at producing them accelerated. I would be working on four reeds at a time, cutting and adjusting each of them every morning and every evening. Many of these reeds hit the trash can, but the ones that survived the process came into performance-ready shape in about a week. Furthermore, I liked the tone quality that cane from large-diameter tubes produced.

I took some of these reeds along with me to see Brian Terrell, Quality Control Manager at Rico International (a 45-minute drive from my house), who has been a friend of mine since we attended Reseda High School together. I always enjoyed talking shop with Brian, and he was pleased to check these new, extra-long reeds on one of Rico's spring-tension gauges. It turned out that two of the four reeds had a stiffness measurement of 2 1/2, and the other two reeds were just a bit less than that (remember that I had started out with cane graded at a stiffness of 3 1/2).

On another occasion, I heard that Arnold Brilhart was on assignment at Rico, so I went over to see him. I had met Arnold before at Elmer Beechler's mouthpiece factory (also nearby) and valued his opinions highly. I brought along my reed-making tools and some finished hand made reeds and spoke to him about my endeavors. He was very favorably impressed with my determination, but his psychology was bent in a different direction than mine. Arnold was most interested in mass-produced reeds and mouthpieces. Here he was, sitting in a factory that produced reeds by the thousands while speaking to a fellow whose best efforts produced a maximum of four reeds per week. As friendly as he was, I could sense his mixed feelings about the subject. I did get some excellent advice about mouthpiece-facing curves from him, though; and this advice made the trip well worth its while.

But mouthpiece experiments would have to take second place. I was still being driven to find more secrets about saxophone reeds.

During another period of deep contemplation, I made another breakthrough in my way of thinking about reeds. Nearly everyone, I am sure, has seen charts and pictures of reeds with notations about where to cut a reed to create some specific effect. In fact, I had drawn many of them myself. But suddenly, this no longer made complete sense to me. I came upon the unavoidable conclusion that every little bit of wood and water affected every note and physical force present in the instrument, not just those to which I had been paying attention at that particular time.

This was a startling and stimulating realization to me, and I knew that my next series of experiments would clear up many questions about reed mechanics.

The problem, as I now conceived, was that regardless of the large amounts of carving my reeds were undergoing, I was still being too timid with my adjustments. The forces of nature are unconditional and will manifest even though only a few bits of wood are removed by a piece of sandpaper or whether a Grand Canyon-sized gouge were sliced with a knife. The results would always be the same. It would be only a matter of the degree of change determined by the amount of wood removed from that particular spot.

I had a drawer full of leftover reeds that I was now going to put to good use. These were reeds of all kinds, good reeds, bad reeds, alto, tenor, and even some clarinet reeds for good measure.

The first series of cuts encompassed the upper heart. An absolutely ridiculous amount of wood was sliced from this area in each of about a dozen reeds. As I knew would happen, the strength declined, the tone became thinner, and the pitch went flat on every single reed without exception. Next, I pulled a fresh batch of reeds and began clipping their tips about 1/16" at a time until they were nearly unplayable. Once again, the results were predictable. The strength increased, the tone became thicker, and the pitch became sharper, also on every single reed without exception. This was really interesting because other things were happening with these reeds; particularly, all the reeds in these series had the length of their bites shortened. I was so intrigued with this process that I took out a sheet of paper and started listing all the physical forces that I could think of or discover, even though I had to make up names for some of them to help keep my thinking straight.

I kept on with the deep slicing experiments. By dividing the blades into six sections, three across for the upper blades and three across for the lower blades, I could systematically gouge different areas for each series of reeds and record my findings on sheets of paper.

I stayed at these procedures for an absurd amount of time. But even though I had not finished the project, my previous speculation had been confirmed. That is, it is impossible to adjust only one force in a reed at a time. No matter where in the blade of a reed that wood may be removed or no matter how large or small the removal might be, every single force in the reed would be changed to some degree. The solution to the mystery of the saxophone reed was now right before me, written on these sheets of paper and supported by a trash can filled with destroyed reeds. And it appeared that proper reed shaping could control of all these forces with the exceptions of excess warping tendencies and poor-quality cane.

This had little effect in the method in which I designed my reeds. But with the knowledge gained in discovering and organizing all the physical forces involved, my thinking had become much clearer. For example, if I were to thin or thicken the bite-line or shoulder measurements (one at a time) by as little as one thousandth of an inch, the results would more predictable than ever before. These results would include the tone/strength/intonation force group, the actions of the primary and concave warps, and the aspects of proportioning, all at one time. There was one significant change to my method, however. I began developing ideal measurements for the lower blade instead of plotting and cutting each reed separately. The lower blades were also becoming much thinner than before to accommodate the short-bite mouthpiece facings that I became to favor.

Looking back upon things, now, the total reed-cutting experience has been a curious adventure. I had started out to perfect and replicate the reed manufacturers' specifications for more consistency and greater blowing comfort. But I wound up preferring something more advanced; that is, reeds that are warp-relieved, microbalanced, and proportioned to match my own embouchure and blowing style.

At this time I wish my skills in physics and mathematics were stronger. If so, improvements in the theories might be found. But someone else will have to do this research because it is beyond my abilities to do so. I am a musician, not a scientist or an engineer. I am grateful to have spent my life making music, and the fulfillment of being the best player I can be is all that I really wanted all along.

❖　　　❖　　　❖

PHOTO GALLERY

❖ ❖ ❖

From Steven D. Harris' Book, <u>The Kenton Kronicles</u>,
Dynaflow Publications, PO Box 60421,
Pasadena, CA 91116-6421, p. 244

❖   ❖   ❖

California club date in '65. (Photo courtesy of Ray Reed)

Ray Reed

"What do I remember most about my time on Kenton's band? My lip hurt for three years!"

179

Playing Marty's Great Chart
On "My Old Flame" in
Santa Ynez, CA, 1993

❖ ❖ ❖

Photo Courtesy of Marty Paich

Supersax at Carmelo's
Sherman Oaks, CA, 1985

L to R: Jay Migliori, Ray Reed, Med Flory (Leader),
Lanny Morgan, and Jack Nimitz

❖   ❖   ❖

Photo Courtesy of Bernie Mather

Relaxing in London's Savoy Hotel
After a Supersax Trip to Spain, 1988

❖   ❖   ❖

Photo Courtesy of Jack Nimitz

Checking Out My Supply of Reeds
Before a Video Shoot With
Steve Wilkerson's "Shaw 'Nuff" Band, 1999

I would usually carry four fully balanced reeds with me along with a few quick-cuts. Each fully balanced reed would be played for about one hour or one set before changing to another fully balanced reed. Rotating reeds in this manner helped to prevent excess water soaking and maintained a long reed lifetime. With four reeds available, I could play up to four sets at a time.

❖   ❖   ❖

Photo Courtesy of Andrea Baker

A Letter of Friendship

Multi-reed instrumentalist Ray Pizzi has been my friend since the late 1960s, having played on several bands together since that time. Ray makes his own bassoon reeds, and this makes it easy to speak with him about saxophone reeds.

Actually, I showed him only a few simple things about saxophone reed adjustments. First, I explained about constructing and using a tip-edge profiler (he decided to nail the feeler gauge to a piece of flat wood). Next, I explained how to reset the upper-blade angle. Then I gave him a clipboard. The rest may be attributed to his own doing.

Ray Pizzi is also an accomplished artist with a keen eye, a steady hand, and a good imagination. I am very pleased to have received this drawing from him.

P.S. Go ahead and play the reeds, Mr. Pizzi.

❖　　❖　　❖

Original artwork entitled "Good Vibrations"
Courtesy of Ray Pizzi, 1995

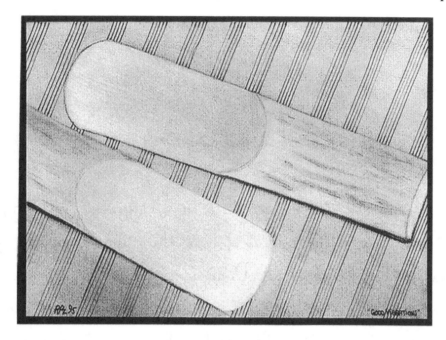

Hi Ray,

Hope you enjoy my art work.
Believe it or not, you were the
inspiration for this piece. I
followed your instructions explicitly,
and "voila" the 2 BEST REEDS
I EVER MADE, what a shame they
can't be played! However, thanks
to you, are discussions have helped
me understand what makes them work
and I'll always appreciate the advice
you gave me.
Thanks for your friendship and your
soul... Best, Ray Pizzi

An Unexpected Gift

While visiting Stein's music store in Hollywood one day, the owner, Gary Chen-Stein, gave me a handful of reeds that came from one of Stan Getz' tenor sax cases. These reeds are all Vandorens, No. 3 1/2. Stan was a truly great tonemaster and one of the most imitated players of all time. Studying these reeds may provide some insight into how he achieved his unique sound.

Two of the reeds shown have pencil marks on the tips and lower corners to indicate some type of speculated cutting. Three of the reeds have the number 14 written on their backs while one other has the number 13. The last reed shown has additional comments penciled on it.

There are 17 reeds in this collection, and none shows any sign of actually having been played. A few of them, however, have evidence of a light smoothing on their backsides. My guess is that this was done on a sheet of notebook paper.

Four of the reeds are contained in a Vandoren holder made of blue plastic. The others are contained in various cardboard holders.

❖　　❖　　❖

| Pencil Marks | Pencil Marks | 14 | Before 16 15/80 |

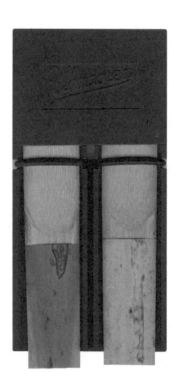

My Collection of Fully Balanced Alto Reeds

These 21 reeds (I have a few more) are all hand made, extra-long, and cut from Rico 3 1/2 baritone or Vandoren 3 1/2 tenor reeds. The crosswise pencil marks are ligature lines.

I tried another experiment to see if it might be possible to establish a separate supply of fully balanced reeds for each month or season of the year. When a month ended, I would place any leftover reeds into storage until the same month in the following year. The results were disappointing. It seems that too many well-used reeds have a tendency to rot in the box when stored for a year or two or three. It would have been better to have played them for their full lifetimes when they were first brought into the working supply.

This brings up another subject. I have hundreds of unused factory-cut alto reeds from the 1970s when the cane quality was far superior to anything available today (to my knowledge, that is—I haven't tried everything). These reeds have maintained their well-centered, snappy sound. But the extra decades of drying out have caused activity in primary warps that are beyond my abilities to repair. I have heard people say they wish they had saved as many boxes as possible from those days. A better wish would be to have some brand-new reeds made from that same-quality cane.

❖　　❖　　❖

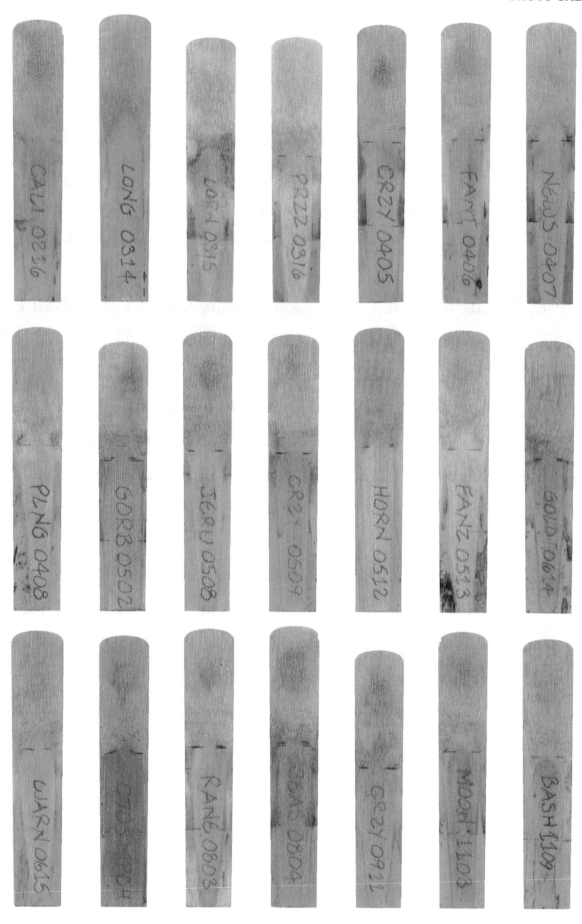

A Personal Choice

There has been much discussion about the best way to store and carry reeds. Nearly everyone, it seems, has at least some small opinion about it.

My favorite is to store hand made rotators loosely in a padded box so that both sides of the reeds may dry out evenly. The box lid is secured with a No 64 rubber band. Double-sided holders; such as, those made by Vandoren and La Voz, are convenient for my quick cuts because when placed into use, they will become keepers and stored wetly on the mouthpiece for their entire lifetimes. The holder is just a practical way to carry the reeds around until they are placed into use.

Many people believe that a flat-clamping holder will keep a reed from warping and curving around the mouthpiece facing. But this is not the whole story. Flat holders without air vents can cause the reed front side to dry out faster than its backside, which may be an unneeded contribution in the warping actions of certain reeds. Curves around the mouthpiece facing are easily handled by an upper-blade-angle reset.

❖　　❖　　❖

NOTES

NOTES

NOTES

NOTES

NOTES

NOTES

Made in United States
Troutdale, OR
06/15/2024

20593549R00133